insight text guide

Scott Hurley

A View from the Bridge

Arthur Miller

insight®

▸innovative ▸engaging ▸evolving

First published in 2004. Reprinted 2009, 2010, 2012, 2020.
Reprinted with revisions in 2024.

Insight Publications Pty Ltd
3/350 Charman Road
Cheltenham VIC 3192
Australia
Tel: +61 3 8571 4950
Email: books@insightpublications.com.au

www.insightpublications.com.au

National Library of Australia Cataloguing-in-Publication entry:
Hurley, Scott.
A view from the bridge - Arthur Miller.
For senior secondary English students.
ISBN 9781920693596
1. Miller, Arthur, 1915-. View from the bridge. I. Title.
812.52

Cover design: The Modern Art Production Group

Printed in Australia by Ligare Book Printers

Insight Publications acknowledges the Traditional Custodians of the Country on which we meet and work, the Boonwurrung People of the Kulin Nation. We pay our respects to their Elders past and present, and extend that respect to all Aboriginal and Torres Strait Islander peoples.

contents

CHARACTER MAP

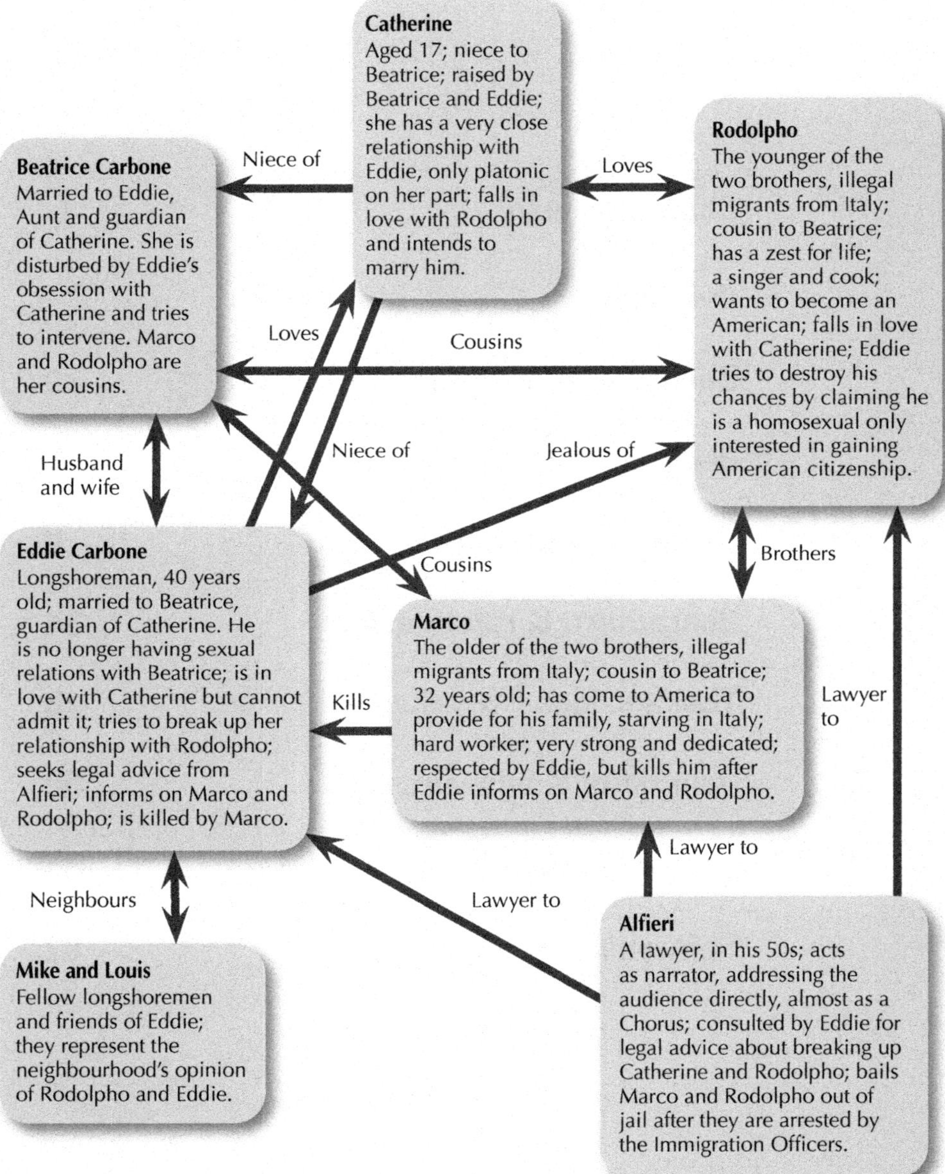

OVERVIEW

A View from the Bridge tells the story of Eddie Carbone, a hard-working longshoreman (stevedore) in New York supporting his wife, Beatrice, and her orphaned niece, Catherine. Tensions arise when Beatrice's cousins, illegal migrants from Italy, come to live with the family, and are further intensified when one of them begins a romance with Catherine. Unable to confront his own, improper feelings for her, Eddie spirals into a course of rage, bullying and venomous accusations. He is lured by his jealousy to commit the ultimate crime in his small Italian neighbourhood: the betrayal of members of his own family. This sets in motion a series of consequences Eddie could not have predicted, including his own destruction when he tries to win back his reputation.

A View from the Bridge is a play about obsession and bigotry, love and jealousy, honour and social position. It is the psychological exploration of how a man unravels when his repressed desires are displaced into hostility and paranoia. It is also the tragedy of a genuine, platonic love destroyed by sexual tension. *A View from the Bridge* is not a play that manufactures suspense from an unpredictable plot; rather, it generates in its audience the kind of horror reserved for those powerless to prevent a catastrophe they must watch unfold from beginning to end.

Arthur Miller was one of America's greatest playwrights. Born in 1915, Miller wrote such classics as *The Crucible* (1953) and *Death of a Salesman* (1949), two of the outstanding plays of the twentieth century. *A View from the Bridge* was first performed in 1955 on Broadway. It began as an experiment, a one-act reaction against the 'psycho-sexual romanticism' Miller saw as dominating the contemporary theatre. As the play moved from its birth in New York to its next incarnation in London in 1956, an evolution occurred (brought about mostly by new possibilities and new limitations in staging). *A View from the Bridge* transformed from a clinical, detached presentation of the protagonist's self-inflicted catastrophe to a complex character study and, not unlike *Death of a Salesman*, the tragedy of a family. It is a fascinating reminder that *drama* does not truly exist until it becomes *theatre*.

BACKGROUND & CONTEXT

Setting

A View from the Bridge is set in Red Hook, Brooklyn, New York City, in the 1950s. Red Hook is a working-class neighbourhood primarily inhabited by longshoremen who work the docks unloading the cargo ships that come into New York Harbor. Though Miller's dialogue captures an authentic Brooklyn accent, the setting of the play is not critical to the action or the themes. Eddie Carbone's occupation does not have so great an influence on how he thinks or behaves that it could not be substituted for some other difficult, uncertain manual labour. Your appreciation of the play does not depend on knowing the ins and outs of a worker's life in Red Hook, circa 1950. This is not true for Elia Kazan's *On the Waterfront*, say (a film on which Miller reputedly worked in the early stages), which shares the exact setting of *A View from the Bridge* but does indeed depend on political and cultural aspects of place and time. However, with regard to Miller's play, it is enough to know that Eddie must work hard to make a living, and that he feels a strong need to maintain his standing in a small, insular community.

Migration

While Miller's play *The Crucible* has political ramifications essential to its meaning (involving the McCarthyist anti-Communist 'witch hunts' of the late 1940s and early 1950s), *A View from the Bridge* does not. It is true that one of the primary catalysts of its plot, illegal immigration, is a major social and political issue both in contemporary Australia and the United States. Miller takes pains to inform us that Eddie's own father migrated to the US from Italy (about half a century before the time in which the play is set), for reasons no doubt the same as those of Marco and Rodolpho or any of the other 'submarines' (illegal immigrants) of Red Hook. But he would have come at the height of an 'open door' policy in the United States, when thousands of migrants from Europe were being processed daily at New York's Ellis Island, and were only sent back in the case of health concerns. The men of Marco's generation face perhaps worse hardships in postwar Italy than Eddie's father would have in his time, yet the door is now closed.

While there is no doubt that Miller wants us to think about this difference, the play never tackles the issue of immigration policy beyond using it as a context through which the plot can unfold. Its strongest impact on themes of the play pertains to local opinion. Eddie's is just one of many families in Red Hook harbouring kin from Italy. When he eventually betrays them to the authorities, he is committing a crime as much against the codes of his entire community as against Marco and Rodolpho. And it is the power of ancient social codes that this play is about, rather than the specifics of public policy.

Arthur Miller on *A View from the Bridge*

Some older Penguin editions of this play begin with an introduction by Arthur Miller; unfortunately, the current edition does not retain it. While many authors' introductions can leave one with more questions than answers, Miller's is refreshingly revealing about how the version of the play we know was brought to life. Its more important insights are worth considering. Originally a one-act play, *A View from the Bridge* was not well received when it opened on Broadway. However, it met greater success in London about a year later when it was presented as the two-act play you have read. Miller calls the one-act New York version 'hard, telegraphic, unadorned drama', and writes that he did not want any of the conventional concerns of theatre to get in the way of the audience's witnessing Eddie's path to catastrophe:

> It seemed to me then that the theatre was retreating into an area of psycho-sexual romanticism, and this at the very moment when great events ... cried out for analytic inspection ... the spectacle of still another misunderstood victim left me impatient ... To bathe the audience in tears, to grip people by the age-old methods of suspense, to theatricalize life, in a word, seemed faintly absurd to me, if not disgusting. (Miller 1977, p.vi)

In other words, his first version probably contained too much 'analytic inspection' for most people, and not enough emotion. In trying to avoid 'heart-wringing sympathy' in favour of 'wonder', Miller seems to have left his first audiences a little cold. The second version was fleshed out by the addition of 'significant psychological and behavioral detail' to become, in his view, 'more human, warmer and less remote' (Miller 1977, p.x).

The role of suspense

The difference between the two versions of the play is really of little interest to us, but what Miller says about his intentions in the first version, and how he met them in a different way in the second, offers a lot of insight into the play's meaning. The idea behind telling Eddie's story as he did in the first version was to limit the theatrical convention of suspense. Miller did not want his audiences' involvement with *how* the story would end to interfere with an appreciation of what it all *meant*: '[Eddie's story] must be suspenseful because one knew too well how it would come out... by knowing more than the hero the audience would rather automatically see his life through conceptualized feelings' (Miller 1977, p.vii).

In the second version, the 'narrative' speeches by the character Alfieri leave little doubt that the play will end tragically, even if he offers no specific details. And even though there is equally little doubt that Eddie is going to make his fatal phone call, a palpable sense of suspense is still generated. Miller is arguing, and I think the play bears it out, that the suspense on offer is of a different kind, intellectual rather than emotional. Rather than *weep* for Eddie, we *wonder* how a man could destroy lives in a cause he cannot properly recognise, and how such a thing could be allowed to go so far when the outcome seemed so predictable. We are not awed by the power of fate or of mercurial gods as we are in classical tragedy; we are awed by something we know only too well: the destructiveness of human emotion.

Another important idea Miller raises has to do with what would seem a minor incident: he was able to hire a larger cast for the London production of the play. The latter scenes could therefore be played before a crowd, and this seems to have crystallised Miller's thinking about Eddie:

> The mind of Eddie Carbone is not comprehensible apart from his relation to his neighborhood, his fellow workers, his social situation. His self-esteem depends upon their estimate of him, and his value is created largely by his fidelity to the code of his culture. (Miller 1977, p.viii)

The addition of a crowd, and of a set that suggested the density of urban living, gave one the sense, in Miller's words, 'that Eddie was living out his horror in the midst of a certain normality, and that invisibly and without having to speak of it, he was getting ready to invoke upon himself the wrath of his tribe' (Miller 1977, pp.viii–ix). I believe this concept is crucial to understanding the very last scenes of the play, when against all sense, and against all recognition of the terrible things he has done, Eddie goes in front of his community to demand back from Marco his reputation, his good name that has been torn down. Bear these comments in mind as you think about and re-read *A View from the Bridge*.

GENRE, STRUCTURE & STYLE

Since *A View from the Bridge* is a play, reading it can only give you part of the picture. That is, a *play* does not fully take life until it is presented as a *production* in which a director and actors make decisions about how lines are to be delivered, how scenes are to be staged and a thousand minor details that can affect the audience's reaction. As you read the lines of the play, always try to keep in mind how it might be staged, and what contribution non-verbal aspects of the play should be making to the overall conception. I have discussed above the fact that *A View from the Bridge* was originally a one-act play that Miller transformed later into the two-act version we now know. The first act is significantly longer than the second, and each uses the same set. There is really little *dramatic* purpose in putting the intermission where it is – although it seems the most logical place to put it, considering that the play is probably too long to run without it.

A modern Greek tragedy?

A View from the Bridge is a tragedy, reminiscent more of classical Greek tragedy than of Shakespearean tragedy. Greek tragedy has some basic concepts that will be useful in helping us to understand *A View from the Bridge*. Greek tragedies portray the downfall of characters larger than life – kings, queens, princes, princesses, or great heroes, some of whom are semi-divine. If their downfalls often are partly due to an intervention by the gods, they also involve what has come to be known as the 'tragic flaw', or in Aristotle's term, *hamartia*. A protagonist's *hamartia* is a blind spot, a mistake or personality flaw that drives this character towards a disaster otherwise preventable. The Greeks' concepts of fate and freewill were complex; suffice to say that they had no problem accepting seemingly contradictory ideas. For instance, in Greek tragedy a tragic hero's downfall is both ordained by fate *and* contingent upon the hero's actions – hence it is directed by the gods, but dictated by the hero's *hamartia*.

The hero's reversal of fortune

In the course of the tragedy the hero experiences a *peripeteia*, or a reversal of fortune. It might be a seemingly innocent event that sets off a chain of others taking some time to unfold, but it invariably ends in catastrophe. Eventually there occurs in the tragic hero an *anagnorisis*, or recognition of the reversal of fortune. Greek tragedies were meant to instruct and the stories were well known. Greek audiences did not attend tragedies to find out what happened, but rather to learn something from the playwright's treatment of a familiar story.

Catharsis

The final term we should discuss, then, is *catharsis*, a release of the pent-up emotion the audience members experience as they watch the tragedy played before them. Aristotle wrote in his *Poetics* that a tragedy should invoke *horror* and *pity* in the audience; they should be horrified at watching the downfall of the hero, but they should feel pity when the hero experiences their own recognition of what has happened. The term catharsis has been adopted into everyday English, and our meaning for catharsis is not much different from Aristotle's: it invokes the idea of a challenging experience that somehow makes us better by surviving it. Again, Greek tragedy was supposed to instruct and not just entertain; catharsis is essentially a transferral of anxiety into higher understanding.

Reading the play as a tragedy

Arthur Miller's introduction has alerted us to some of the ways we might see *A View from the Bridge* as a modern version of Greek tragedy. It definitely involves a reversal of fortune in the life of its main character, as well as a notable tragic flaw that leads irrevocably to Eddie's downfall and death. The biggest problem we might have with such a reading is the fact that Eddie is hardly a 'great man', not a king or a hero but a common longshoreman from an undistinguished neighbourhood in Brooklyn. Miller observed that an important aspect of the London production of the play was that Eddie's tragedy was able to unfold before a large crowd representing his neighbourhood:

> A certain size accrued to him as a result. The importance of his interior psychological dilemma was magnified to the size it would have in real life. What had seemed like a mere aberration had now risen to a fatal violation of an ancient law. (Miller 1977, p.ix)

The severity of Eddie's abuse of the code by which the people of Red Hook live makes him somehow larger, more mythic than he might have been.

However, Eddie still does not match the profile of a classical tragic hero. What Miller does not mention is a trend in twentieth-century art that sought to demystify some of the codes of classical literature and reapply them to modern life. Arthur Miller was one of its great exponents; his *Death of a Salesman* is the perfect example of the tragedy of an ordinary man, proof that a salesman's life is as rich a subject as a king's for the tension and emotionality of high tragedy. Many other artists explored these ideas in their own ways – Eugene O'Neill in his tragedies, Irish novelist James Joyce in his epic *Ulysses*, even the composer Aaron Copland (who was born in Brooklyn) in the piece of music entitled 'Fanfare for the Common Man'. I suspect that it is *because* Miller was a leading exponent of this literary movement that he does not defend his right to make tragedy out of the story of an obstinate longshoreman. Certainly, though, a tragic dimension does accrue to this working-class man who destroys himself through jealousy and desire.

Miller's words about not wanting to appeal to his audience's emotions would seem to fly in the face of Aristotelian catharsis, yet if 'pity' is missing, *A View from the Bridge* is not short on 'horror'. More to the point, Miller's goal of getting his audience to respond to the work intellectually is precisely the same as that entailed by the Greek concept of catharsis. He was simply trying to achieve this result (of an enhanced understanding) without capitalising on the audience's emotions in ways so prevalent in the theatre he decries: 'the tender emotions, I felt were being overworked' (Miller 1977, p.vi). Similarly, Miller's determination to eliminate the element of suspense is consistent with the ideals of Greek tragedy. Though Eddie's story is not familiar to his audience before they sit down to a performance, the play almost behaves as if it were, thanks to the foreboding speeches of Alfieri, the lawyer.

Alfieri as Chorus figure

Alfieri is probably the closest link in *A View from the Bridge* with Greek tragedy, because he essentially fills the role taken by the Chorus in classical theatre. The Greek Chorus is composed of varying numbers of people who have roles both *within* the action of the play, and outside it, addressing the audience directly in the latter. They discuss occurrences in the play, ruminate over the intercessions of the gods or enhance the audience's appreciation of the playwright's themes in reflective, speculative language. Their role is complex, but it might not be too simplistic to say that the Chorus's function is to *explain* one thing or another.

Alfieri is the perfect modern equivalent of a Chorus, a man who takes part, to a limited extent, in the action of the play, yet who addresses the audience in speeches that are by turns evocative of Miller's themes, or that are full of portent about the unfolding tragedy. Indeed, Alfieri's presence itself lends a tragic air to the proceedings that the events of the play *themselves* might not evoke until the end of the long first act. To audiences familiar with the elements of Greek tragedy, Alfieri's opening address, as well as his deportment and gravity, is tantamount to an announcement: 'You are about to see a tragedy, everybody!'

Realism

One aspect of the play's style that does mark a substantial difference between *A View from the Bridge* and Greek tragedy is its use of realism. Though modern interpreters are free to do what they like, ancient Greek theatre originally relied on highly stylised performances, on artifice rather than believability: characters wore enormous masks that were anything but lifelike; they probably stood stock still as they declaimed their lines loudly enough for a large audience to hear. The Chorus *sang* their lines and accompanied them with ritualised, dance-like movements.

By contrast, Arthur Miller's plays are the height of twentieth-century realism. No line exists that does not sound natural and perfectly believable coming from the mouths of working-class people from Brooklyn or Sicily. Nothing happens that we feel is implausible, with the important exception of Alfieri's talking to the audience. This is the only device Miller uses to break the feeling that we are witnessing 'real life' unfold before us. Yet it does not interfere with our acceptance of the play's action as a 'real' story; rather, we accept Alfieri's interjections as a convention, as the best way for us to gain knowledge of events that have already occurred. There are also other motives for having Alfieri speak directly to the audience, which I will address elsewhere in this text guide.

Miller's use of realism is not at all inconsistent with our calling *A View from the Bridge* a modern tragedy. Rather, it is an element in his strategy of creating twentieth-century tragedies with common people, rather than exalted personages, as protagonists. If ancient Greek tragedy strives to demonstrate aspects of the human condition by using dramatically exaggerated, grandiose figures, then it stands to reason that it also relies on high artifice to create even more distance between what occurs on stage and what occurs in the everyday lives of its audiences. It is like a sermon delivered from on high.

The tragedies of Arthur Miller, on the other hand, require total believability for their impact; they encourage audiences to identify not with what they would like to be, but with what they are, or at least with the kind of people who share their own world. Ultimately, there is little difference in result: just as we need not be a king to be personally affected by the tragedy of Oedipus (in Sophocles' *Oedipus the King*), neither do we need to be a longshoreman to be affected by Eddie Carbone's tragedy. If the intellectual and emotional benefits of tragedy are like medicine, then the stylistic elements of a playwright, or an era, or a production, are just the ways that the medicine is delivered. The tragedy can be conveyed in any number of ways; what really matters is that we get the benefits.

SCENE-BY-SCENE ANALYSIS

Though *A View from the Bridge* is not formally divided by scenes (only by acts), it is clear where scene breaks occur, based on a change of location or time, the entry or exit of characters, the fading and bringing up of lights, etc. To facilitate analysis, I have given these scenes numbers and treat them separately.

Act One

Scene 1 (pp.11–13)

Summary: *A description of the set and an introduction to the lawyer Alfieri.*

Most of the action of *A View from the Bridge* takes place in the tenement 'worker's flat' where Eddie Carbone and his family live. Stage directions call for the whole building to be visible. In his notes to the play, Miller describes the set constructed for Peter Brook's 1956 London production:

> [it] soared to the roof with fire escapes, passageways, suggested apartments, so that one sensed that Eddie was living out his horror in the midst of a certain normality, and that, invisibly and without having to speak of it, he was getting ready to invoke upon himself the wrath of his tribe. (Miller 1977, p.viii)

Key point

Bear these words in mind as you read the play. The fact that Eddie is 'living out his horror' in the plain sight of a close and crowded community is crucial to understanding so many of the decisions he makes.

The lawyer Alfieri addresses the audience, introducing Red Hook as 'the gullet of New York, swallowing the tonnage of the world' (p.12), immediately presenting himself as a kind of narrator for the story to come. This device was fairly experimental in 1955, but is more common now. Alfieri is the only character who will transgress the conventions of realistic theatre in this way, and we are entitled to ask why – a question I address in more detail in the Characters & Relationships section. Alfieri's unique position adds another dimension to Eddie's 'living out his horror' in the plain view of his community. Though he is a member of that community, Alfieri's role as narrator links him more strongly with the audience. Alfieri is telling us that, though he will play some role in the proceedings, he is as 'powerless' as the audience to intervene as Eddie's tragedy 'run[s] its bloody course' (p.12).

Scene 2 (pp.13–25)

Summary: *Eddie, Beatrice and Catherine discuss Catherine's offer of a job and the arrival that evening of Beatrice's cousins from Italy.*

This scene offers a glimpse into the existence the three characters maintain before the entrance of the cousins from Italy. Eddie and his wife, Beatrice, have been caring for her niece Catherine since the latter's mother died when Catherine was a baby. It is a close household. Catherine (now seventeen) is eager to please Eddie and Bea, fetching him a beer or a cigar, helping her set the table. From the beginning of the scene, Eddie betrays a combination of adoration and overprotectiveness towards Catherine: he admires her dress, but wonders if it is too short; he recognises that she is growing into a beautiful woman, but criticises her for 'walkin' wavy' on the street (p.14). Citing his promise to her mother that he would take of her, he wishes Catherine would be less friendly. Notice the contradictions in his assertions: he calls her a 'baby' who doesn't 'understand these things', but in practically the next breath says she's 'getting to be a big girl now' (pp.14–15).

Eddie changes the topic by announcing that Beatrice's cousins from Italy will arrive that night. They have been smuggled into the country by a syndicate, and will be staying with Eddie and Beatrice until they can find a place of their own. Beatrice is very nervous about the arrangement, not because of the illegality of harbouring illegal immigrants, but because of the tension it might create with Eddie. For his part, Eddie is worried about Beatrice; he says that she is so generous that he is afraid she'll be pushed around. This mini-dispute offers Eddie a chance to explain the way he regards the great favour they will be doing for the Italian cousins:

> It's an honor B. I mean it. I was just thinkin' before, comin' home, suppose my father didn't come to this country, and I was starvin' like them over there… and I had people in America could keep me a couple of months? The man would be honoured to lend me a place to sleep. (p.17)

These are fine sentiments, even noble ones. The arrival of the cousins will of course create tensions of a magnitude none of them could foresee, yet for all of the retrospective irony we might later attach to this speech, there is no reason to suspect that Eddie does not mean it. Beatrice is moved to tears and calls Eddie 'an angel', assuring him that God will bless him for his generosity (p.17).

It is a day of big news. The arrival of the cousins is not the only thing happening; Catherine has been offered a job as a stenographer for a plumbing company. About this news, Eddie is less philosophic; he refuses to give his approval, using a series of arguments that suggest his objections have less to do with worries for her than with his own loss of control over her life. Beatrice challenges him while Catherine is out of the room: 'I don't understand you; she's seventeen years old, you gonna keep her in the house all her life?' (p.20). Eventually Eddie relents, but it is not clear whether Beatrice's argument has won the day, or the sight of Catherine returning to serve dinner, the style of her hair making her look to Eddie 'like a madonna' (p.20). Either way, he gives her some grave advice about people: 'Believe me, Katie, the less you trust, the less you be sorry' (p.21).

Key point

This episode serves two important purposes. First, it introduces the idea that Eddie's overprotectiveness of his niece runs much deeper than his rather trivial concerns about Catherine's 'wavy walkin''. Second, rather than alluding to divisions in the family, the episode underscores just how well they are able to resolve their differences. The issue of Catherine's working is difficult for Eddie, yet he relents with relative good grace, and there is no lingering ill will among them. In other words, early in the play, before the arrival of the cousins, Miller paints a portrait of a close family whose members care about each other, who worry about each other, who disagree but do not allow it to come between them. Things will soon be very different.

The conversation soon returns to the imminent arrival of the cousins. Eddie cautions Beatrice and Catherine not to say anything to anybody about their house guests. He tells the terrible story of Vinny Bolzano, a teenager who informed to the Immigration Bureau on an uncle and who was beaten and spat upon in the street by his family as a result. Eddie draws this conclusion about him: 'You'll never see him no more, a guy do a thing like that? How's he gonna show his face? ... you can quicker get back a million dollars that was stole than a word that you gave away' (p.24). Much like Beatrice's earlier insistence that Eddie would be blessed by God for taking such a kindly attitude to the arrival of her cousins, these words might send a shudder through the *re*-reader of *A View from the Bridge* who knows the actions Eddie will later take.

Scene 3 (pp.26–33)

Summary: *Marco and Rodolpho arrive at Eddie's flat and describe something of their lives.*

Alfieri makes a brief appearance that does little other than indicate that an hour or so has passed. He summarises Eddie's life to this point in the following way: 'He was as good a man as he had to be in a life that was hard and even' (p.26). By intruding again in this fashion Alfieri reminds us that he is telling us a story whose end has already been determined, even if we are only witnessing its beginning. Such reminders help to defuse the kind of identification that theatre audiences almost instinctively make with the protagonist of a play.

Q Why would Arthur Miller want to achieve this effect?

Beatrice's cousins arrive, and the difference between them is immediately apparent. While Marco is dark, sturdy and strong, Rodolpho has blond hair and a slight build. Marco is quiet and formal; Rodolpho is animated, familiar and outgoing. Marco seems much more comfortable talking to Eddie than to the women, and he makes a point of thanking him, specifically and more than once, for the sacrifice the family is making; Rodolpho is immediately attentive to the women. Though Marco, as the older sibling, initially takes the lead in introducing himself and his brother to their American relatives, soon Rodolpho is doing all the talking, explaining how difficult their life has been in Italy, but in a way that is remarkably devoid of bitterness. He is humorous and optimistic; he can see the comical side of their hardships, and seems full of high hopes about his future in America. Marco, though, is clearly weighed down by responsibility, since he has a wife and three children to support in Italy. He has taken the extraordinary course of migrating illegally to the United States out of desperation: 'What can I do? ... My wife – she feeds [the children] from her own mouth. I tell you the truth, if I stay there they will never grow up' (p.29).

'Paper Doll'

For his part, Rodolpho reveals that he wants to become an American, to stay permanently. Yet he also dreams of returning to Italy rich enough to buy a blue motorcycle; with a motorcycle, he can become a messenger! It is the kind of nonsensical plan that only youth and exuberance could hatch, qualities that Rodolpho embodies. Soon Catherine is hanging on his every word; when he reveals that he is also a singer and knows one of her favourite songs, she demands that he sing it. However, Eddie interrupts Rodolpho's performance of 'Paper Doll', saying that the singing might attract the attention of Immigration Bureau informants.

The lines of the song immediately preceding his interruption, concerning 'flirty, flirty guys / With their flirty, flirty eyes' (p.32), suggest Eddie's real motive: he is trying to break the spell under which Catherine is falling. Her reaction – 'Leave him finish, it's beautiful ... He's terrific! It's terrific Rodolpho' (p.32) – suggests that it is too late. Eddie tries to assert his control over Catherine by making her change out of the high heels she is wearing, but the scene ends with Eddie's realisation ('*his face puffed with trouble*', stage direction, p.33) that Catherine has fallen for the blond Italian cousin.

Scene 4 (pp.33–8)

Summary: *Eddie and Beatrice avoid discussing the sexual problem they are having; Eddie waits for Catherine and Rodolpho to return from the movies; Eddie talks about the cousins with his friends Mike and Louis.*

Alfieri addresses the audience again to tell us that a few weeks have passed since the previous scene. He also says that 'Eddie Carbone had never expected to have a destiny' (p.34). What does he mean by this? It is a way of reinforcing a point that Alfieri has been making in each of his speeches, that Eddie was just a normal man, the kind who 'works, raises his family, goes bowling, eats, gets old, and then he dies' (p.34). Catherine's infatuation with Rodolpho, it is suggested, is the triggering event that will alter Eddie's existence from that of a typical longshoreman into something about which tragic, cautionary tales like Alfieri's are woven.

Eddie is waiting out on the street for Catherine and Rodolpho to return from the movies when Beatrice enters, and Eddie initiates a conversation about the two. He is only vaguely hostile to Rodolpho until Beatrice says that he's a 'nice kid'; this prompts a tirade from her husband on Rodolpho's faults: he sings on the ships, which makes the other longshoremen laugh at him; he has 'wacky hair' (p.34). These opinions seem fairly harmless, but Beatrice senses that Eddie is going to use them as an excuse to try to break up Catherine and Rodolpho. Her suspicion is validated by Eddie's response to her command that he doesn't 'start nothin'': 'I ain't startin' nothin', but I ain't gonna stand around lookin' at that. For that character I didn't bring her up' (p.35).

Without addressing these remarks, though, Beatrice latches onto something else Eddie says: 'I sit there waitin' for you to wake up but everything is great with you' (p.35). She refers to a different sore point in their relationship: they have not had sex for three months and everything is not 'great' with her. Eddie refuses to talk about it other than to say that 'I don't feel good, that's all' (p.36). We are starting to fill in the pieces of Eddie's psyche: he is being extremely protective of his beautiful adopted daughter, wanting to keep her at home, attacking the character of the young man she has fallen in love with. He is also not having sex with his wife. What has all this to do with the special 'destiny' that Alfieri has attributed to Eddie? This remains to be seen.

The opinions of Louis and Mike

Beatrice does not push Eddie for an explanation; she goes inside while Eddie talks to Louis and Mike, who have appeared on the street. They are soon discussing Eddie's 'submarines', Marco and Rodolpho. Louis and Mike admire Marco for his strength and his attitude to work, whereas Rodolpho they call 'funny', and soon they are both in hysterics as they try to remember some of the funny things that the younger brother has said. Nothing in the remarks of Louis and Mike indicate, definitively, that they are making fun of Rodolpho, but that is certainly the way Eddie takes it. Miller has left this brief interaction ambiguous, and one can imagine the scene being played very differently in different productions.

Q What do you think? Are Mike and Louis laughing *at* Rodolpho, or are they laughing *with* him?

Either way, Eddie is convinced that they are laughing at Rodolpho and that they share his low opinion of the young man. Notice, however, that Eddie actually supports Rodolpho in front of his friends, offering the same explanation for his peculiarities that Beatrice gave to him: 'he's a kid yet, y'know?' (p.37).

Key point

At this point in the play, Eddie is still a man who closes rank around family, no matter what he thinks of them.

Scene 5 (pp.38–42)

Summary: *Eddie confronts Catherine about Rodolpho and insists that he is only using her to become an American citizen.*

When Catherine and Rodolpho return late from the movies, Eddie is suspicious that they might have gone into Manhattan (they call it New York); Eddie has forbidden Rodolpho to take her to Times Square. Of course Rodolpho is dying to go there and see the lights of Broadway in person. Here we see a fundamental difference between these two male characters: Eddie, who has lived all his life in New York City, thinks that Times Square is a place only for 'tramps', while Rodolpho has in his mind an image of Times Square as the most romantic place in the world.

After Rodolpho leaves them, Eddie grills Catherine to find out how strongly she feels about the young man. When she affirms that she 'likes him' (p.40), Eddie is devastated. He insists that Rodolpho does not respect her, because if he did he would have asked Eddie's permission before he started dating her (p.40). After Catherine defends him, Eddie moves to heavier artillery, asserting that Rodolpho is only interested in Catherine as a ticket to getting his citizenship: 'The guy is lookin' for his break, that's all he's lookin' for' (p.41). This attack proves more effective than the previous one.

Key point

This is a turning point, a moment when Eddie abandons his role of a guardian who is 'looking out' for Catherine, for something else, because here, rather than merely interpreting what he sees in Rodolpho, he undertakes a deliberate 'smear campaign' against him – it seems more like the tactic of a jealous lover.

Scene 6 (pp.42–5)

Summary: *Beatrice gives Catherine some advice about her conflict with Eddie.*

Eddie and the sobbing Catherine enter the apartment. Beatrice is there, and after she angrily warns Eddie to leave Catherine alone, Eddie leaves the apartment to the two women. Beatrice takes this opportunity to tell Catherine that Eddie will never approve of any man she falls in love with. More than his willingness to break up Catherine's romance, what alarms Beatrice is the degree to which Catherine is affected by it:

> You still think you're a little girl, honey. But nobody else can make up your mind for you any more, you understand? You gotta give him to understand that he can't give you orders no more. (p.43)

Beatrice tells Catherine that she must stop acting like a child around Eddie – including walking around in her slip, or talking to him while he's shaving in his underwear. Beatrice recognises that there is an unhealthy sexual energy between her husband and her niece but Catherine is not even aware of it. In order to protect both of them, Beatrice insists that Catherine say 'good-bye' to the child who grew up under Eddie's care, and become a woman who makes her own decisions (p.44). Catherine agrees to try.

Scene 7 (pp.45–50)

Summary: *Eddie seeks legal advice about Rodolpho from Alfieri.*

One afternoon soon after the previous scene, Eddie seeks advice from Alfieri about what he can do to stop Catherine from marrying Rodolpho. Alfieri tells the audience that Eddie's 'eyes were like tunnels', and that a 'passion… had moved into his body, like a stranger' (p.45). Then the conversation he has with Eddie is played out before us. Eddie begins by telling Alfieri the same thing he had told Beatrice, that Rodolpho is spending too much money – on records and clothing – to be intending to do anything but stay permanently in the United States. When this has no effect on the lawyer's position that there is nothing he can do about it legally, Eddie reveals something he was not willing to tell Beatrice, that he thinks Rodolpho is homosexual, though he is too embarrassed to say this in anything but the most roundabout way.

What is Eddie's evidence for this assertion? That Rodolpho is blond, that he is of slight build, that he sings and can hit some pretty high notes (as a tenor should, of course), that he altered one of Catherine's dresses for her to make it fit better. It is the litany of the true homophobe; all of it is meaningless, a product of Eddie's ignorance and bigotry. Alfieri tells Eddie that even if his suspicion is correct, there is nothing in the law that says Rodolpho cannot marry Catherine, a proposition that Eddie simply cannot accept: 'You mean to tell me that there's no law that a guy which he ain't right can go to work and marry a girl and – ?' (p.47). Alfieri says the only legal question pertains to how the brothers entered the country, but Eddie shies away from this question immediately. Concerned only with breaking up Rodolpho and Catherine, he declares that he would never consider informing on his wife's cousins to the Immigration Bureau.

Satisfied that he has dissuaded Eddie from trying to take legal action against his lodger, Alfieri offers some personal advice to Eddie: he has too much love for Catherine, and this is blinding Eddie from taking the correct course of action. Alfieri urges Eddie to: 'Let her go ... You did your job, now it's her life; wish her luck, and let her go' (p.48). This good advice is not very different from that given to Eddie by Beatrice in Scene 4, and one senses that Eddie could save himself and go back to being a man without a 'destiny' if he would only heed it. Instead, Alfieri's words seem to spark in Eddie a recognition of what is really troubling him about the situation: it is not Catherine who is being wronged, but Eddie himself.

Eddie's sacrifices for Catherine

Eddie recalls how hard he has worked to bring up his niece, how he has had to 'hustle' when there was no work: 'I took out of my own mouth to give to her. I took out of my wife's mouth. I walked hungry plenty days in this city!' (p.49). He concludes that Rodolpho's putting his 'dirty filthy hands' on Catherine has nothing at all to do with her wellbeing; rather, 'He's stealing from me!' (p.49). Alfieri sees the truth behind Eddie's anger, and confronts him with it, saying 'She can't marry you, can she?' (p.49). Eddie's fury indicates how deeply these words strike him; clearly what disturbs Eddie so much about Rodolpho and Catherine is that Eddie himself is in love with her, yet he cannot bring himself to admit it.

Alfieri ends this scene with another address to the audience detailing his feeling that he knew exactly the fate that awaited Eddie, down to the last detail, but that he was powerless to do anything about it.

Key point

In this speech, we see why Miller chooses to let Alfieri speak to the audience: the feelings he describes are precisely those of an audience at a tragic play. As audience members, we witness the protagonist setting the course of his destiny through his own failings, and we watch him come to his tragic conclusion bereft of the power to do anything about it.

Scene 8 (pp.50–8)

Summary: *A strained evening at home ends the first act: Catherine and Rodolpho dance; Eddie and Rodolpho box; Marco quietly warns Eddie.*

Having revealed the full extent of Eddie's feelings about Rodolpho, Miller immediately puts his protagonist into the kind of claustrophobic domestic setting for which he is famous. Knowing what we have learned in the previous scene, we can only see Eddie as a powder keg waiting for the spark that will set it off.

The scene opens benignly with an amiable conversation about the brothers' experiences working on fishing boats in Italy. Even Eddie participates, with an unintentionally comical assertion: 'I heard that they paint the oranges to make them look orange' (p.51). But he becomes hostile when Rodolpho tries politely to correct him. When the conversation turns to his wife in Italy, Marco assures everyone that she will remain faithful to him while he is away. Eddie sees this as an opening to make a point about the allegedly disrespectful way Rodolpho has gone about courting Catherine, that he is keeping her out 'on the street' sometimes until midnight (p.53). It is not a particularly strong argument, and after an attack by Beatrice ('the movie ended late'), he changes it: 'If he's here to work, then he should work; if he's here for a good time then he could fool around!' (p.54). This reveals two things: that Eddie is not very committed to his assumed role as protector of Catherine's virtue, and that he is using it as an opportunity to express his general dislike of Rodolpho.

In 'revolt' against Eddie's statement, Catherine puts on a recording of 'Paper Doll' and asks Rodolpho to dance with her. This is the song Rodolpho sang in Scene 3, and one Catherine knows will hurt Eddie. Beatrice steers the conversation back to fishing boats. However, following Marco's comment that everybody enjoys it when Rodolpho works on the boats because he is such a good cook, Eddie sees another opening to attack the young man: 'It's wonderful. He sings, he cooks, he could make dresses' (p.55). As though '*exposing the issue*' (stage direction), Eddie says that if he himself could do all those things, he would not be 'on the water-front', but 'in a dress store' (p.55). To Eddie's reckoning this innuendo could not be clearer – he is all but accusing Rodolpho of being a homosexual.

A round of boxing

Before waiting to see what the response will be, Eddie changes the subject to boxing; he invites Marco to the 'bouts' on Saturday night, then uses the opportunity to offer Rodolpho an impromptu boxing lesson. In the course of this lesson, predictably, Eddie lands a significant blow, staggering Rodolpho. After it is over Eddie says to Marco that: 'He could be very good, Marco. I'll teach him again' (p.57). Marco suggests a friendly contest of his own, between himself and Eddie, which results in Marco proving that his strength is greatly superior to Eddie's. Holding a chair over Eddie's head '*like a weapon*' (stage direction, p.58), Marco demonstrates that he has seen through Eddie's little performance, and is silently warning him that there will be consequences if he tries to bully his brother again.

Consider how well this scene is choreographed. The underlying tension existing between Eddie, Rodolpho and Catherine, though it never presents itself overtly, bubbles to the surface in the form of three cases of physical interaction between two characters:

- Catherine and Rodolpho's dance
- Eddie and Rodolpho's 'boxing lesson'
- Marco and Eddie's contest of strength.

Eddie's verbal attack against Rodolpho's character results in Catherine dancing with Rodolpho. Almost as if he were attempting to 'cut in on' this dance (but on the female rather than the male) he proposes his boxing lesson with Rodolpho. Just as Catherine's dance was a way for her to get at Eddie, Eddie's lesson is intended to prove to Catherine that Rodolpho is not a 'man' at all. Failing to do this initially (Rodolpho is better at boxing than Eddie thought he would be), Eddie contents himself with landing a blow to Rodolpho, and warns that he 'will teach him again'. But Marco shows that he too possesses a 'dance card'. In a sense he 'cuts in on' Eddie's 'dance' by challenging him to the chair-lifting contest; he knows what Eddie is up to, and will not let him get away with it. Rodolpho responds to the boxing lesson in his own way, by immediately returning to Catherine and initiating the resumption of their dance to 'Paper Doll' (remember, he had been reluctant to offend Eddie by dancing with Catherine earlier in the scene). The scene is masterfully plotted by Miller: although the facade of domestic civility (if not quite domestic bliss) has been maintained, hostilities and alliances have been forged, challenges have been laid down, and there is no doubt that the parties know exactly where they stand.

Act Two

Scene 9 (pp.59–63)

Summary: *Rodolpho and Catherine find themselves alone in the house for the first time, two days before Christmas.*

Alfieri appears again to address the audience. What he has to reveal could easily have been worked into the ensuing dialogue between Catherine and Rodolpho, so we should again recognise that the lawyer is there because Miller wants him to be there. He is reminding us, again, that the story of Eddie Carbone and his family is coming to us secondhand, that it has occurred in the past.

Alone together in the apartment for the first time, Catherine confronts Rodolpho with the issue that has been troubling her since Eddie suggested it in Scene 5: is Rodolpho only interested in her to gain his passport? She seeks his answer in a roundabout way, by asking him if he would still want to marry her if it meant living in Italy (p.60). His response, that he would have to be crazy to bring her back to Italy, is not what she expects. She would like Rodolpho to give her a romantic answer – that he would live with her in Italy or anywhere, just as long as he could be with her. But his answer is pragmatic. To return with her to Italy, where they would both risk starving, would be 'criminal' (p.60). Moreover, Rodolpho senses that Catherine's question has not really come from her, but from Eddie, and this makes him furious: 'Do you think I am so desperate? My brother is desperate, not me. You think I would carry on my back the rest of my life a woman I didn't love just to be an American?' (p.61). It really is the answer Catherine was looking for after all.

Having made his case, Rodolpho demands to know why Catherine is so afraid of Eddie. She does not want to hurt the man she has looked up to all her life, a man she knows better than his own wife does:

> I can tell a block away when he's blue in his mind and just wants to talk to somebody quiet and nice … I know when his feet hurt him, I mean I know him and now I'm supposed to turn around and make a stranger out of him? (p.62)

In response, Rodolpho compares Eddie to a man who holds a bird he loves tightly in his hand, refusing to let it fly: 'I don't say you must hate him; but anyway you must go, mustn't you? Catherine?' (p.63). She now puts all of her faith and trust in Rodolpho, saying 'I don't know anything, teach me, Rodolpho, hold me' (p.61).

Rodolpho's instinct is to lead Catherine into the bedroom, a development that would have been more shocking to audiences in the 1950s than it may seem now.

Q How do you judge Rodolpho's move: is it an act of love, or is he trying to capitalise on Catherine's confusion?

Scene 10 (pp.63–5)

Summary: *A drunken Eddie returns, interrupting Catherine and Rodolpho; he kisses Catherine and again tries to prove that Rodolpho is a homosexual.*

Hearing Eddie's return, Catherine comes out of the bedroom, adjusting her dress. Rather than hide in the bedroom, Rodolpho appears in the doorway, telling Eddie that no-one else is in the house, and thus essentially announcing what he and Catherine have been up to. Eddie's response is abrupt and decisive: 'Pack it up. Go ahead. Get your stuff and get outa here' (p.63). When Catherine moves to leave too, Eddie stops her, saying 'you ain't goin' nowheres, he's the one' (p.64). Catherine seems finally to resolve in her mind what she must do, telling Eddie that she 'just can't stay here no more' (p.64). When she insists that she is not going to be a 'baby' any more, Eddie cuts her off by kissing her forcefully on the mouth.

Key point

This aggressive sexual gesture underscores the threat behind Eddie's 'you ain't goin' nowheres'. Yet it is also the inevitable culmination of his relationship with her over many years, equal parts adoration and domination. It is most telling that he tries to assert sexual control over her at the moment she says she will no longer be a baby: keeping her a 'baby' is precisely the way he has tried to control her until now.

Rodolpho breaks them up with a shout of 'Have respect for her!' (p.64). His words ironically highlight the reversal of his and Eddie's relationship with Catherine, for until now Eddie has insisted that it is Rodolpho who has been disrespectful. When Rodolpho states that Catherine will be his wife, Eddie challenges him with 'what're you gonna be?' (p.64), a new version of the same old accusation, that Rodolpho is a homosexual who could not possibly fulfil the role of husband. (Keep in mind the hypocrisy of this comment, when Eddie knows that he is not fulfilling his wife's sexual expectations.) When Rodolpho moves to attack him, Eddie pins his arm and kisses Rodolpho aggressively on the mouth just as he had done to Catherine. Now it is Catherine who breaks them up, threatening to kill Eddie. His response to her, 'You see?' (p.65), indicates that the kiss was Eddie's final, bizarre attempt to prove Rodolpho's homosexuality, and he is convinced that it has worked.

We might remember Eddie's observation to Alfieri in Scene 7, that when Rodolpho had altered Catherine's dress 'he looked so sweet, like an angel – you could kiss him he was so sweet' (p.47).

Q What should we make of this? Does Eddie have repressed homosexual feelings for Rodolpho, or is it just that a sarcastic comment made earlier has given Eddie an idea about how finally to expose his adversary?

Eddie's homophobia

Eddie is undoubtedly classically homophobic, a condition that can hint at repressed homosexual desire. Remember that his drunkenness makes him more likely to act on impulse. Also, perhaps Eddie's desire for Catherine has been strangely electrified by her desire for someone else, so that it somehow extends even to his rival. These are interesting possibilities, but I think the strongest possibility is the simplest: Eddie is so ignorant of homosexuality that he really believes a kiss from a man, even one as frightening and repulsive as Eddie is in this scene, must elicit some kind of sexual response in a homosexual man. Regardless of Eddie's motives, consider how shocking this scene would have appeared to Miller's original audiences – it is scarcely less so today. The scene ends with Eddie extending his threat to Rodolpho even to Catherine herself: 'Don't make me do nuttin', Catherine' (p.65). With his two kisses, Eddie seems to realise that he has lost Catherine forever; nevertheless, he does not intend to let Rodolpho have her.

Scene 11 (pp.65–7)

Summary: *Eddie returns for another consultation with Alfieri.*

Alfieri informs the audience that Eddie returned to his office four days after the incident detailed in the previous scene. Alfieri again describes how helpless he felt as he witnessed Eddie's tragedy unfold: 'it occurred to me how – almost how transfixed I had come to feel' (p.65).

Contrary to Eddie's orders, Rodolpho and Marco are still living in the apartment. Beatrice has been making inquiries about finding them another place to stay upstairs, but nobody is saying anything about the events of the previous scene. Alfieri insists that Eddie did not prove anything with his kiss, but Eddie is still convinced that Rodolpho 'ain't right'. It is turning into a kind of *idée fixe* with Eddie; despite all evidence to the contrary, he is convinced of Rodolpho's homosexuality. Of course, his conviction is merely an excuse to pursue an end that he cannot bring himself to admit: by breaking Catherine and Rodolpho up, he will be able to keep Catherine at home, all to himself. He uses an interesting image to counter Alfieri's contention that Rodolpho was simply not strong enough to break Eddie's grip: 'Somebody that don't want it can break it. Even a mouse, if you catch a teeny mouse and you hold it in your hand, that mouse can give you the right kind of fight' (p.66).

Key point

Though Eddie is ostensibly talking about Rodolpho, consider how fitting a description it is of Eddie's relationship with Catherine herself. She is the 'mouse' that Eddie is trying to hold in his hand – and his entire objection to Rodolpho is actually a response to the 'kind of fight' Catherine is now giving him to being held. Each of Eddie's actions represents an increasingly desperate attempt to hold on tightly to his 'teeny mouse'.

Convinced in his mind that he has proved his point, Eddie asks Alfieri what he should do now. The lawyer's response starts rather cryptically: 'the law is nature. The law is only a word for what has a right to happen' (p.66). He is trying to say two things: that Eddie has no case whatsoever under the law, and, more important, that Eddie is acting in a way that is unnatural. His desire for Catherine, while not definably incestuous, goes against the natural order. He has raised her from a baby, sacrificed for her and loved her; now it is time to 'Let her go. And bless her' (pp.66–7). But this seems to be something that Eddie's desire will simply not allow. Alfieri recognises the extent of Eddie's desperation, anticipating where it will lead him next. As a phone booth begins to glow across the stage, the lawyer warns Eddie, without saying so directly, not to inform on Beatrice's cousins: 'Even those who understand will turn against you, even the ones who feel the same will despise you!' (p.67).

Scene 12 (p.67)

Summary: *Eddie calls the Immigration Bureau to inform on Marco and Rodolpho.*

Despite Alfieri's advice, Eddie makes the call from the phone booth and informs on Beatrice's cousins. Mike and Louis happen on the scene, as they often do, and ask Eddie if he would like to go bowling. Their presence should reinforce the import of Alfieri's last words – people like Louis and Mike may indeed agree with Eddie about Rodolpho, but what Eddie has just done will be seen by them, and the community, as the worst imaginable crime. Remember Eddie's own words about Vinny Bolzano: 'You'll never see him no more, a guy do a thing like that? How's he gonna show his face?' (p.24).

Scene 13 (pp.67–77)

Summary: *Marco and Rodolpho are arrested by Immigration Officers.*

Eddie returns home after his phone call to find Beatrice alone in the apartment. She tells him that Catherine has moved her cousins into an empty room in an apartment upstairs. When he insists that Catherine 'ain't movin' in with them', Beatrice explodes: 'Look, I'm sick and tired of it... I wish I'd a drop dead before I told them to come' (two different speeches, p.68). Eddie uses this as an opportunity to assert his position in the household, demanding that Beatrice respect him. It is quite an involved conversation, a very realistic depiction of the kind of dispute between a wife and husband that can jump rapidly from topic to topic without either member getting lost. All the issues coming between them – from Eddie's treatment of Catherine to his treatment of Rodolpho, to his lost desire for Beatrice, to his perception that she 'attacks' him all the time with her opinions – all the things that they have been unwilling to talk about come tumbling out. When the topic comes around to Catherine's welfare, though, the two stop arguing. Beatrice tells Eddie that Catherine and Rodolpho are getting married next week, and that he should try to restore his relationship with her before they do. Her statement that she thinks Catherine still loves him (p.70) affects Eddie deeply, bringing him to tears, but he cannot face Catherine.

When Catherine herself appears in the apartment, Eddie grabs his jacket to go for a walk, but Beatrice holds him back, forcing the two to speak to each other. Catherine invites him to the wedding, to this response: 'Okay. I only wanted the best for you, Katie. I hope you know that' (p.71).

Q Do you think Eddie is being sincere?

An innocent request by Catherine for extra pillowcases reveals that there are two other 'submarines' in the apartment where she has put Marco and Rodolpho. Eddie panics, telling Catherine that she has to get the cousins out of the house. Of course, Eddie fears the retribution that will fall on his head if the Immigration Officers come to the house and arrest the two other men, who are relatives of Lipari the butcher and his family. He cannot say that he has already called the Immigration Bureau, so he creates a scenario in which one of Lipari's enemies might have informed on them: 'These guys get picked up, Lipari's liable to blame you or me and we got his whole family on our head' (p.73). There is no reason to doubt his sincerity when he tells Catherine 'never mix yourself with somebody else's family' (p.73). If he at least gets Marco and Rodolpho out of the house before the immigration authorities arrive, then there will be no connection to them when Lipari's relatives are picked up. But before this can be achieved, there is the expected knock at the door, and after a brief search, Marco, Rodolpho and the two other men are arrested by two officers.

Marco and Rodolpho are arrested

As this is happening, Beatrice realises how the Immigration Bureau has come to know about the submarines, screaming at Eddie: 'My God, what did you do?' (p.74). Beatrice and Catherine then plead for the men's release as they are being led from the apartment. Marco takes advantage of the opportunity to hang back a little and then run back into the apartment to spit in Eddie's face (p.75). Eddie loses all control, threatening Marco: 'I'll kill you for that, you son of a bitch!' (p.76). He follows the officers and their captives into the street, where a crowd has gathered, including Lipari and his family.

Key point

Miller paints a striking contrast between these two families: as Lipari silently kisses his relatives, Eddie continues screaming at Marco: 'That's the thanks I get? Which I took the blankets off my bed for yiz? You gonna apologize to me, Marco!' (p.76).

Q Recall Eddie's earlier words about what an honour it is to help out family in the way he has helped Marco and Rodolpho. Do you think these words were genuine? If so, then how have things come to this?

While one of the officers is busy dealing with Catherine, who continues to plead for Rodolpho, Marco takes the opportunity to explain, in front of the neighbourhood, exactly why he spat in Eddie's face: 'That one! He killed my children! That one stole the food from my children!' (p.77). As

Lipari and the crowd begin to turn away from Eddie, the full import of Marco's accusation becomes apparent to him; almost pleading, Eddie tries to persuade Lipari, and then Louis, that he kept Marco and Rodolpho 'like [his] own brothers'. As the scene ends, Eddie is left alone, insisting that he will kill Marco for his accusation (p.77).

Scene 14 (pp.77–80)

Summary: *Alfieri, Rodolpho and Catherine try to convince Marco not to do anything to Eddie.*

This scene takes place in '*the reception room of a prison*' (p.77). Alfieri is there to bail the brothers out, but not until Marco promises that he will not attempt to harm Eddie. At first Marco refuses to make this promise, saying that in Italy Eddie would already be dead for his treachery. Rodolpho and Catherine work on him; they are going to get married, and Rodolpho wants his brother to be at the wedding. Catherine further tells Marco that what awaits Eddie is going to be a Red Hook version of his Italian fate: 'Nobody is gonna talk to him again if he lives to a hundred' (p.78). She also points out that Marco could keep working, and continue to send money back to his family, during the weeks it will take for his case to come to court. This argument affects Marco, but he still does not want to do something dishonourable. Alfieri says that: 'To promise not to kill is not dishonorable' (p.79). Marco then asks what will be done with Eddie, expecting that the law will be on his side. He is stunned when Alfieri responds: 'Nothing. If he obeys the law, he lives' (p.79).

The nature of justice and the law

This exchange is reminiscent of the discussions Eddie has had with Alfieri about Rodolpho. Just as Eddie could not believe there was no legal recourse to prevent Catherine's marriage to a man who 'ain't right', Marco cannot believe there is no law to invoke against a man who informs on his own family. Once again Alfieri is there to defend the law, but once again he does so in a way that his interlocutor finds unsatisfying:

> MARCO [*rises, turns to* ALFIERI]: The law? All the law is not in a book.
> ALFIERI: Yes. In a book. There is no other law.
>
> MARCO [*his anger rising*]: He degraded my brother. My blood. He

> robbed my children, he mocks my work. I work to come here, mister!
> ALFIERI: I know, Marco –
> MARCO: There is no law for that? Where is the law for that?
> ALFIERI: There is none. (p.79)

As Marco seems to be yielding for the sake of his brother and his children, Alfieri takes one of Marco's hands, indicating that it is a potential weapon that should not be used: 'This is not God, Marco. You hear? Only God makes justice' (p.79).

Scene 15 (pp.80–3)

Summary: *Back in the apartment, Eddie refuses to let Beatrice attend Catherine's wedding; the latter confronts him, but they are interrupted by Rodolpho who tells them Marco is coming.*

Beatrice, dressed in her best clothing, is about to leave when Eddie tells her something he has clearly been saying all day: 'You walk out that door to that wedding you ain't comin' back here, Beatrice' (p.80). Beatrice pleads with him to let her go for the sake of her sister (Catherine's mother). Catherine enters and angrily attacks Eddie: 'You got no more right to tell nobody nothin'!' (p.80). Calling him a 'rat', she continues to undermine Eddie's authority by telling Beatrice how much she despises him: 'He bites people when they sleep! He comes when nobody's lookin' and poisons decent people. In the garbage he belongs!' (p.81). When Eddie looks likely to commit an act of violence, Beatrice steps in to defend her husband, telling Catherine that: 'Whatever happened we all done it, and don't you ever forget it, Catherine' (p.81).

Q Is this true? What responsibility do Beatrice and Catherine bear for the events that have transpired?

Rodolpho enters the room to announce that Marco will soon arrive, that he is presently praying in the church. This is an ominous sign; Marco must be praying to ask forgiveness from God for some violent action he is intending to commit. Rodolpho, Catherine and Beatrice each take their turn pleading with Eddie not to be there when Marco arrives. Rodolpho apologises for everything that has happened in the hope that if he patches things up with Eddie, Marco might not kill him. But Eddie is unmoved by their protestations. When Beatrice asks him what he wants, Eddie roars:

'I want my name! [Rodolpho] didn't take my name; he's only a punk. Marco's got my name' (p.82). He tells Rodolpho that if Marco does not give Eddie back his name 'in front of this neighbourhood', then they are going to 'have it out' (p.82).

Recall Eddie's comment to Catherine in Scene 2, in relation to the story of Vinny Bolzano: 'Just remember, kid, you can quicker get back a million dollars that was stole than a word that you gave away' (p.24). Now, at the end of the play, Eddie is trying to get back the word that he gave away with his phone call, but as if in denial about what really occurred, he seems truly to think that Marco *stole* his name. The most important part of Eddie's formulation is that it all occur 'in front of this neighbourhood', for no matter how he has come to this juncture, Eddie knows he does not have a future in Red Hook unless he can regain the standing he has lost.

Beatrice tries a last, desperate ploy, confronting directly the one issue about which they cannot speak. She says that even if Marco did give Eddie back his name, it would not be enough, since: 'You want something else, Eddie, and you can never have her!' (p.83). She finishes by saying: 'The truth is not as bad as blood, Eddie!' (p.83); finally the truth has come to the surface in direct words rather than innuendo or suggestion. Beatrice says what no-one has been willing to talk about, that all of Eddie's actions have been responses to a sexual desire for Catherine that he knows is wrong, that is indeed *so* wrong that he has not been able even to admit its existence.

Scene 16 (pp.83–5)

Summary: *Marco calls to Eddie from the street; they fight and Eddie dies.*

Marco arrives, calling out 'Eddie Carbone!' (p.83). People from the neighbourhood gather around; as Marco's accusation occurred before them, so too will the conclusion to the conflict. Eddie puts his case to the crowd: 'I put my roof over their head and my food in their mouth' (p.83). He recites his litany of grievances against the brothers, including Marco's accusation, then he addresses Marco: 'Now gimme my name and we go together to the wedding' (p.84). But this is not really the resolution that Eddie wants, for he keeps baiting Marco, calling him a 'liar'. Of course Marco has no intention of backing down; he is there to avenge himself on the man who has 'killed [his] children' (p.77).

When Eddie lunges at Marco, the latter clubs him to the ground with his fist. Eddie pulls out the knife he has hidden in recognition of Marco's superior strength. Louis's interference here ('Eddie, for Christ's sake!', p.84) is another chance for Miller to portray the opinion of the crowd. It is a gesture of condemnation: Eddie is not fighting fairly; even if he were to win, there is no way he can regain his name now. Eddie essentially acknowledges this in the way he threatens Louis momentarily with the knife before turning to Marco. He is beyond saving, and he knows it. Marco yells 'Anima-a-a-l' (p.84), an accurate description, for Eddie is acting now like a cornered animal; he cannot talk his way out of this, will never win back his name, will never win back Catherine. He lunges with his knife, but Marco grabs his arm and, turning the blade inward, plunges it into Eddie.

Key point

This denouement is symbolic of Eddie's actions throughout the play: he has killed himself – with his bullying and his paranoia, with his inappropriate desires, with his informing and his accusations – and correspondingly dies by his own knife.

As he is dying, Catherine cries out: 'Eddie, I never meant to do nothing bad to you' (p.84). He begins to respond as though to shift the blame for his own actions onto her yet again: 'Then why – '. But he thinks better of it, realising that his time is at an end, and realising, too, what he is really losing: 'Oh B.! ... My B.!' (p.84).

Alfieri closes the play by addressing the audience for the last time. He begins by reiterating a line from his first speech: 'Most of the time now we settle for half and I like it better' (p.85). It is a strange way to say it, but Alfieri is telling us that we live in a world now where reason or temperance, or even indifference, tend to succeed over the emotions that cause the kind of disaster we have just witnessed. For all his faults, Eddie was somehow 'perversely pure', 'he allowed himself to be wholly known'. There was no middle ground with Eddie; his loves, his jealousies, his hatreds were all of an intensity that one rarely sees in our modern world. This makes Alfieri realise that he loves Eddie 'more than all [his] sensible clients', even as he acknowledges that it is 'better to settle for half' (p.85).

Q What do you think of Alfieri's 'eulogy' for Eddie?

CHARACTERS & RELATIONSHIPS

Eddie

Key quotes

[About letting Marco and Rodolpho stay with them]

'It's an honour, B. I mean it.' (p.17)

'BEATRICE: You're an angel! God'll bless you…You'll see, you'll get a blessing for this!' (p.17)

'Just remember, kid, you can quicker get back a million dollars that was stole than a word that you gave away.' (p.24)

'ALFIERI: He was as good a man as he had to be in a life that was hard and even.' (p.26)

'ALFIERI: Eddie Carbone had never expected to have a destiny...Now, as the weeks passed, there was a future, there was a trouble that would not go away.' (pp.33–4)

[About his lost sexual attraction to Beatrice] 'I can't. I can't talk about it.' (p.36)

'ALFIERI: His eyes were like tunnels… a passion had moved into his body, like a stranger.' (p.45)

'ALFIERI: The child has to grow up and go away, and the man has to learn to forget.' (p.48)

'I'm a patsy, what can a patsy do? I worked like a dog twenty years so a punk could have her [Catherine] …' (p.49)

'CATHERINE: He was good to me, Rodolpho. You don't know him; he was always the sweetest guy to me. Good.' (p.62)

'The last year or two I come in the house I don't know what's gonna hit me. It's a shootin' gallery in here and I'm the pigeon.' (p.69)

'MARCO: That one! He killed my children! That one stole the food from my children!' (p.77)

'CATHERINE: He's a rat! He belongs in the sewer!' (p.81)

'BEATRICE: You want somethin' else, Eddie, and you can never have her!' (p.83)

'ALFIERI: But the truth is holy, and even as I know how wrong he was, and his death useless, I tremble, for I confess that something perversely pure calls to me from his memory…' (p.85)

As the protagonist of *A View from the Bridge*, Eddie Carbone is the play's most important character. If this is self-evident, it is perhaps less apparent that Eddie is also the play's most complex character. Consider Alfieri's words: 'A man works, raises his family, goes bowling, eats, gets old, and then he dies' (p.34). The words imply simplicity, but when considering Eddie we would be wise not to listen too closely to them. For he does not just become complicated because Beatrice's cousins arrive from Italy. Rather, their arrival is a kind of activating agent that brings to the surface heretofore suppressed qualities of Eddie's personality.

There are, of course, ways that Eddie could be considered simple: he is stubborn and opinionated; the thought that he might be incorrect about something (and he is incorrect about many things) never seems to cross his mind. Such qualities, though common, betray a lack of perspicacity. A phrase from Alfieri's last speech might help us here: he says there is something 'perversely pure' about Eddie (a fine oxymoron), that 'he allowed himself to be wholly known' (p.85). This statement, too, is only accurate to a degree; if we had the power to cross the border between art and life in order to interview Beatrice, I doubt she would agree that Eddie 'allowed himself to be wholly known'. What Alfieri is really describing are those qualities we have already pointed to, namely, Eddie's stubbornness and his perceived infallibility.

Key point

What this intelligent lawyer calls 'pure' about Eddie is the latter's total incapacity for self-analysis, to stand apart from himself and judge his own behaviour, to examine his motives. Indeed, Eddie is the antithesis of self-reflective; he is self-delusional.

If he is unable to make judgements about himself, we readers or members of the audience are not so afflicted, and based on Eddie's tragic demise, we are liable to come to strongly negative conclusions about him. Still, Eddie is not all bad. In fact, this play either stands or falls on Miller's ability to convince us that it is the story of an *admirable* man come to disgrace and death through the agency of a single character flaw: the obsessive protectiveness of his niece Catherine, born of his inappropriate desire for her. To begin with, Eddie should not be considered out of the context of his occupation. It is no mistake that his very first lines relate to his working life (he tells Louis that 'there's another day yet on that ship', p.13). In the very uncertain world of the longshoreman, Eddie 'scrambles' to keep afloat. He works when the work is available, and he looks for it somewhere else when it is not. He takes very seriously his role as provider for Beatrice and Catherine, and if, in the course of the play, he will use the fact that he 'broke [his] back' for Catherine (p.70) to justify contemptible actions, it does not mean that he did not make sacrifices for her.

Nor are all of Eddie's feelings for Catherine inappropriate. On a number of occasions he displays a normal parental pride or affection for her. He has a clear sense of duty beyond his immediate family as well, supplying safe lodgings for Beatrice's cousins, which he initially considers an honour. Even when his jealousy concerning Catherine's romance with Rodolpho is beginning to percolate, he shrugs off Louis's suggestion that he should be commended for his sacrifice (p.37). Yet what is admirable in Eddie becomes perverted by his obsession for Catherine. His sense of satisfaction at being a good provider becomes, in his mind, a point of grievance, and then a weapon to be used against Catherine. His concern for her and Beatrice becomes hectoring then eventually bullying. And in his greatest failing, his sense of duty toward Beatrice's cousins dissolves into his betrayal of them.

His sexual obsession with Catherine is a kind of lens; held up to aspects of Eddie's personality, it either distorts them beyond recognition, or it magnifies them to monstrous proportions. His old-fashioned ideas about his position as head of the household devolve into something like paranoia as he continuously demands 'respect' from Beatrice. His ordinary concerns about appearing well in his community become a raging (and fatal) campaign to force Marco to give him back the 'name' that he no longer deserves.

In order to obtain a more complete understanding of Eddie's character, it is best to analyse his relationships with the other main characters as we discuss them.

Catherine

Key quotes

'EDDIE: I don't like the looks they're givin' you in the candy store.' (p.14)

'BEATRICE: She's got a job.

EDDIE: What job? She's gonna finish school.' (p.18)

[To Eddie] 'BEATRICE: I don't understand you; she's seventeen years old, you gonna keep her in the house all her life?' (p.20)

'EDDIE: With your hair that way you look like a madonna, you know that?' (p.20)

'EDDIE: I guess I just never figured on one thing…That you would ever grow up.' (p.25)

'EDDIE: It's just I used to come home, you was always there.' (pp.39–40)

'BEATRICE: You still think you're a little girl, honey. But nobody else can make up your mind for you any more…You gotta give [Eddie] to understand that he can't give you orders no more.' (p.43)

'EDDIE: What's the matter with you, don't you believe I could think of your good?' (p.73)

'Eddie, I never meant to do nothing bad to you.' (p.84)

Eddie and Beatrice have raised Catherine since the death of her mother, Beatrice's sister Nancy (p.26), when Catherine was an infant. Catherine is not a 'blood relation' of Eddie's, but she is family. One should not forget that he has fulfilled his voluntary commitment as though Catherine were his own daughter. There seems to be no reason to doubt his good intentions for Catherine's future, yet he is clearly overprotective of the seventeen-year-old, not letting her go out and reluctant to allow her to take a job that she wants very badly.

Eddie is by turns worshipful of Catherine, and overbearing; he likens her to a madonna, yet he calls her a baby. Still, for all these mixed signals (perhaps because of them?), Catherine and Eddie seem to be on a wavelength not shared by Beatrice. It is Catherine who knows when Eddie is tired, when he is 'blue in his mind', when he wants a beer or some quiet company (p.62). He is the one with whom she wants to share things. But at the time of her sexual maturity, their relationship seems to have moved to a different level, at least from Eddie's perspective: adoration for the child has turned into sexual love for the budding woman.

The 'Paper Doll' syndrome

Yet Eddie cannot admit even to himself so distressing a development. Though he represses his true feelings, his need to have Catherine to himself is manifested in other ways. He limits her access to life beyond their home and school, ostensibly because it is dangerous; but then calls her a 'baby' because she has no experience of the world. A person's independence comes first from a belief that she can make it on her own. Eddie tries to sabotage such a belief in Catherine before it can begin; he tries to make her dependent upon him not just for money but for her very opinion of herself.

We might call this the 'Paper Doll' syndrome: Eddie bristles when Rodolpho sings this song (Scene 3), because he sees in an instant that he is going to lose Catherine to him. The place at which Eddie interrupts 'Paper Doll' ('And then those flirty, flirty guys / With their flirty, flirty eyes / Will have to flirt with dollies that are real', p.32) is of course ironically relevant to Rodolpho, but the lines that would have followed, had he been allowed to continue, match perfectly Eddie's desire for Catherine: 'When I come home at night she will be waiting / She'll be the truest doll in all the world'. Indeed, Eddie expresses this desire almost exactly when he says to her in Scene 5: 'I used to come home, you was always there' (pp.39–40).

Eddie and Catherine's fraught relationship

Perhaps the central question we should address regarding Eddie's relationship with Catherine is this: how can a man convince himself that he is doing the right thing for someone when he is clearly doing something harmful? In Scene 13, when Catherine questions Eddie's advice about getting Marco and Rodolpho out of the building, Eddie goes on this tirade:

> What's the matter with you, don't you believe I could think of your good? Did I ever ask sump'm for myself? You think I got no

> feelin's? I never told you nothin' in my life that wasn't for your own good. Nothin'! (p.73)

We know that Eddie has informed on the brothers as a response to Catherine's avowal that she is going to marry Rodolpho. In other words, essentially everything Eddie says here is a lie: he cannot really be thinking of her benefit; he is asking quite a lot for himself; he has told her terrible things (lies about Rodolpho, lies about his current motives for wanting them out of the house) that cannot be 'for [her] own good'. But Eddie seems truly to believe the things he is saying. Again, his desire for Catherine is so heinous to his own mind that he cannot acknowledge it; repressed, it manifests itself in ways that eventually lead him to betray both Catherine and his most deeply held principles.

Yet as we condemn his actions in the play let's remember that it was Eddie's willingness to raise and love unreservedly a child not his own that created an atmosphere for this betrayal. Before Eddie's love for a child turned into desire for a woman, he and Catherine seemed to have an amazingly close and loving relationship. The most tragic thing in *A View from the Bridge* is the degeneration of this love into hatred. One might argue that Eddie truly dies some time before his fight with Marco – when his beloved Catherine tells him he belongs 'in the garbage' (p.81).

Catherine's youthful innocence

Catherine's other relationships really serve to highlight just how young and uncertain she is, at least initially. Beatrice instructs her that she has been behaving inappropriately around Eddie, that she needs to remember that she is a woman and no longer a child. Agreeing to this on the surface, Catherine cannot understand why it is she has to 'make a stranger' (p.62) out of the only man she has ever known in her life. It is a fair question, but not a terribly mature one. One senses that she would like to be a woman who yet remains Eddie's 'little girl'. Rodolpho also calls her a 'little girl' (pp.62–3), and her relationship with him seems to differ little from a teenager's crush. But then Juliet was only a teenager, and if Catherine's relationship with her Romeo does not really mature, *she* manages to mature through it. She makes up her mind that she will marry Rodolpho, and refuses to capitulate to Eddie's tactics.

Beatrice

Key quotes

'EDDIE: I just don't want you bein' pushed around, that's all. You got too big a heart.' (p.17)

'When am I gonna be a wife again, Eddie?' (p.36)

'BEATRICE: You think I'm jealous of you, honey?

CATHERINE: No! It's the first I thought of it.

BEATRICE: Well you should have thought of it before... but I'm not.' (p.44)

'CATHERINE: If I was a wife I would make a man happy instead of goin' at him all the time.' (p.62)

'I wish I'd a drop dead before I told [Marco and Rodolpho] to come. In the ground I wish I was.' (p.68)

'It's [Catherine's] wedding. There'll be nobody there from her family. For my sister let me go. I'm goin' for my sister.' (p.80)

'Whatever happened we all done it...' (p.81)

'The truth is not as bad as blood, Eddie!' (p.83)

Beatrice and Eddie's marriage

Beatrice and Eddie express genuine concern for each other in the second scene of the play. Does this concern belie the tension that has cropped up between the two or does it reflect a more true relationship beneath it? It seems that the couple were happily married until the last two years or so (this is the time frame Eddie provides in Scene 13, p.69). In other words, the beginning of their difficulties coincided with Catherine's sexual maturity and her new position as desired object and as rival. Beatrice declares to her niece that she is not jealous of her – and we have no reason to disbelieve this statement. What Eddie defines as Beatrice's 'jumping' him all the time refers mainly to her repeated insistence that Eddie stop sheltering Catherine from the world. It is partly her way of trying to defuse the growing obsession she is witnessing in her husband, but there are other merits to her case. In Scene 13, for instance, Beatrice is able to point out to Eddie the consequences he has reaped for keeping

Catherine isolated – she has fallen for the first man that Eddie could not keep out of her life (p.70).

Beatrice and Eddie have another problem, of course: his loss of sexual desire for her. As he does with Catherine, Eddie redirects a personal flaw into a fault in the related party. Unable to face the reason behind his sexual apathy, he harps on Beatrice's 'lack of respect' for him. This is a different strand emanating from the same problem. Eddie's sexual desire for Catherine has created a gap between husband and wife, manifest in his lost desire for Beatrice and in Beatrice's disapproval of the way he is controlling their niece.

One of the things that best defines their relationship is their inability to talk about things. Eddie cannot talk about his lost sexual desire; Beatrice cannot talk about her recognising his desire for Catherine. Only at the very end of the play will she directly address it: 'You want somethin' else, Eddie, and you can never have her!' (p.83). It is a last ditch effort to save his life, but it comes too late. Still, Eddie's dying word is Beatrice's name – in the end he seems to realise that he has always loved her, and that he has betrayed her in a fundamental way.

Rodolpho

Key quotes

'Me, I want to be an American.' (p.30)

'MARCO: He dreams, he dreams.' (p.31)

'CATHERINE [*enthralled*]: Leave him finish, it's beautiful! ... He's terrific! It's terrific, Rodolpho.' (p.32)

'BEATRICE: He's a nice fella, hard workin', he's a good-lookin' fella.' (p.34)

'EDDIE: You know what they're callin' him now? Paper Doll they're callin' him, Canary.' (p.35)

'MIKE [*starting to laugh*]: Well he ain't exackly funny, but he's always like makin' remarks like, y'know? He comes around, everybody's laughin'.' (p.37)

'I would like to go to Broadway once, Eddie ... Since I was a boy I see pictures of those lights.' (p.39)

'EDDIE: You marry him and the next time you see him it'll be for divorce!' (p.41)

'EDDIE: The guy ain't right, Mr. Alfieri.' (p.46)

Key quotes

'EDDIE: I take my blankets off my bed for him, and he takes and puts his dirty filthy hands on her like a goddam thief!' (p.49)

[To Catherine] 'I want you to be my wife, and I want to be a citizen ... I am not a beggar, and you are not a horse, a gift, a favour for a poor immigrant.' (p.61)

The younger of the two 'submarines', Rodolpho is outgoing, handsome and charming. If Marco is only in Brooklyn to earn enough money to support his family in Italy, Rodolpho is fully committed to becoming an American. He sings and tells funny stories; he wants to do something great.

Rodolpho and Eddie

There is probably a lot of truth to Beatrice's suggestion that no man would ever have been good enough in Eddie's eyes for Catherine, but Eddie seems to take an immediate dislike to Rodolpho, even before it becomes evident that Catherine has fallen in love. Yet the intensity of Eddie's hatred for the young man is fed by his own desire for Catherine – his sense that he must destroy the rival. That Eddie is unable to admit to his desire makes his relationship with Rodolpho even more problematic. The more Eddie denies his true motives for trying to break up Catherine and Rodolpho, the more he imagines Rodolpho to be offensive. Eddie is ignorant enough to believe that any man who can sing, cook and make dresses must be gay, but his accusation of homosexuality is for Eddie the outward sign of Rodolpho's underlying, sinister motives, namely that Rodolpho is just using Catherine to gain an American passport. All of Rodolpho's personality traits – his singing and cooking, his geniality, zest for life and lack of thrift – cohere for Eddie into a unified, guilty verdict.

But the only 'crime' Rodolpho is truly guilty of is the one Eddie cannot even admit exists: he is the man who proves that Eddie can never have Catherine. Eddie would have to destroy the character of any man who came for Catherine; alleging Rodolpho's homosexuality and ulterior motives is the way that he destroys Rodolpho's character, first *in his own eyes* before trying to convince Catherine. Eddie reveals his true position on Rodolpho in one of his complaints to Alfieri: 'He's stealing from me!'

(p.49). What he resents in Rodolpho is that he is taking his 'Paper Doll' from him; unable to admit this, his mind must create other reasons for his feelings of jealousy and betrayal.

Rodolpho's maturity

When Catherine, made suspicious by Eddie's accusations, asks Rodolpho if he would still marry her if they had to live in Italy, we are given a glimpse of the young man's more serious side. He is really quite mature about his ambitions: he will not marry anyone to live with them in poverty. He resents the way Eddie is patronising him, but he also resents Catherine's willingness to believe that he is so desperate to be an American that he would burden himself with a wife he does not love. Rodolpho's speech is a corrective to more than Eddie's and Catherine's suspicions; it is a corrective to the kind of patronising attitudes that so many people share about the men and women who come to countries like the United States and Australia looking to make their lives better.

Marco

Key quotes

'I want to tell you now Eddie – when you say go, we will go.' (p.27)

'What can I do? The older [child] is sick in his chest. My wife – she feeds them from her own mouth. I tell you the truth, if I stay [in Italy] they will never grow up.' (p.29)

'EDDIE: Marco goes around like a man; nobody kids Marco.' (p.35)

'We have many families in our town, the children never saw the father. But I will go home. Three, four years, I think.' (p.52)

[To the Immigration Officers] 'BEATRICE: Who're they hurtin', for God's sake, what do you want from them? They're starvin' over there…' (p.75)

'All the law is not in a book.' (p.79)

'EDDIE: I want my name! [Rodolpho] didn't take my name; he's only a punk. Marco's got my name…' (p.82)

The older of Beatrice's cousins, Marco is thirty-two, strong and hard working, quiet and serious. He has come to America for one purpose: to make money for his family who are starving in Italy. Eddie has a deep respect for Marco. Like him, Eddie has suffered and sacrificed for his family; he admires Marco for this and for his silence and work ethic. Consider the greatest irony about his informing on Marco and Rodolpho, an action that Eddie deludes himself into thinking is in the interest of his family. Rodolpho is essentially untouched (he and Catherine will marry anyway, and he will begin to get his citizenship) but *it will destroy Marco's family*. In his relationship with Marco one can see the *best* in Eddie, in the generosity with which he shares his home for six months – and the *worst*, in the malicious and selfish act that may well condemn Marco's children to starvation.

The intensity with which Marco works is matched by the intensity with which he seeks to redress the wrong Eddie does to him. He spits in Eddie's face, and accuses Eddie of his crime before the neighbourhood. Upon his release he comes for vengeance, though it means forfeiting a chance to earn money for his family while he awaits trial. Not to do so would be dishonourable, just as, for Eddie, not responding would be dishonourable.

Key point

It is only fitting, therefore, that Marco, who shares many of Eddie's positive qualities, should be the agent of Eddie's destruction, after Eddie surrenders to his worst qualities.

Alfieri

Key quotes

'I am inclined to notice the ruins in things…' (p.12)

'And now we are quite civilized, quite American. Now we settle for half, and I like it better.' (p.12)

'There are times when you want to spread an alarm, but nothing has happened…I knew where [Eddie] was going to end. And I sat here many afternoons asking myself why, being an intelligent man, I was so powerless to stop it.' (pp.49–50)

'[T]he law is nature. The law is only a word for what has a right to happen.' (p.66)

[To Marco] 'Only God makes justice.' (p.79)

'But the truth is holy…' (p.85)

As is not the case with any of the other characters, this story could be told without Alfieri. This lawyer is present as storyteller because Miller wants there to be one – and that should be the lens through which we view him. Through Alfieri's repeated assertions of his powerlessness in the face of Eddie's tragic course, Miller achieves two things. The first is technical: he reminds his audience that they are in a theatre, watching a play. As Aristotle asserted more than two thousand years ago, the effects of a tragedy are heightened by the audience's awareness that it is witnessing a tragedy. Alfieri guides us through the seemingly normal life of a longshoreman with enough presentiments of doom that when things do actually start to take a tragic turn, we are primed for it, sensitive and alive to it.

The second thing Miller achieves through the character of Alfieri is thematic. Alfieri's sense of powerlessness also instills in the audience a sense that there can be no other fate for Eddie than the one he meets. Alfieri refers to Eddie's suddenly having a destiny when he never expected one before (p.34). Here is a truism for modern theatre: a character's psychology is his destiny. In other words, Alfieri's position, as the self-aware observer watching Eddie destroy himself, reinforces the idea that Eddie's obsession is too strong to be contained, altered or redirected. It is a kind of fury that will give him no peace until it wreaks the fullness of its vengeance.

Otherwise, Alfieri has some comments about the actions in the play that have the appearance of being sanctioned by the author. Whether this is true or not, we cannot say. For the most part, I see platitudes where Alfieri thinks he is being most profound. I have demonstrated that Eddie is a far more complicated character than Alfieri seems to allow. The lawyer's final remarks are muddled and unhelpful. Alfieri's advice to Eddie is not unsound, but it might be too abstract for a man who thinks there are people to paint the oranges orange (p.51). And Alfieri is taken in completely by Marco's promise not to harm Eddie – perhaps because he is so busy expounding the abstract nature of justice.

The tragic ironies of Eddie Carbone

Tragedies are always laced with irony. Consider some of the ironies to Eddie's story:

- His inappropriate love for Catherine prompts him to behave in a way that pushes her away forever.
- Though he tells Catherine the story of Vinny Bolzano to keep her from telling anyone about Marco and Rodolpho, Eddie himself will emulate Vinny.
- Eddie declares the importance of one's 'word', but gives his away irremediably.
- Eddie must fight to the death the brother he respected, because of his animosity to the other.
- Eddie is killed with his own knife, signifying his destruction by his own hand.

THEMES, IDEAS & VALUES

Justice and the law

Key quotes

'ALFIERI: [I]n Sicily, from where their fathers came, the law has not been a friendly idea since the Greeks were beaten.' (p.12)

'EDDIE: You mean to tell me that there's no law that a guy which he ain't right can go to work and marry a girl and – ?' (p.47)

'ALFIERI: [T]he law is nature. The law is only a word for what has a right to happen.' (p.66)

'MARCO: All the law is not in a book.' (p.79)

'ALFIERI: Only God makes justice.' (p.79)

Let's begin with Alfieri's first speech. He talks about his legal practice, remembering the days when Red Hook was the testing ground for gangsters like Al Capone, and he dwells on the less romantic lives of the longshoremen he deals with now. But every once in a while, he says, a case comes along that could have occurred in ancient times ('some Caesar's year', p.12) – the kind of timeless catastrophe that seems far from modern America and more the provenance of the blood feuds of southern Italy. Alfieri is telling us that Eddie Carbone's story is going to involve just such a catastrophe, one in which the lawyer, whether ancient or modern, can only watch, 'powerless' as it runs its 'bloody course' (p.12).

We will discuss this feeling of powerless observance below; what Alfieri is saying about the law is another matter: Eddie's case is one in which the *law itself* is powerless, because the main players – Eddie and Marco – act according to principles they believe are outside the (written) law. Eddie has deluded himself, through ignorance and jealousy, into thinking that Rodolpho is a homosexual; but he is truly flabbergasted when Alfieri tells him there is no law to prevent a homosexual from marrying a woman so that he can get his citizenship. Marco is equally astounded when Alfieri tells him that there is no law to redress the wrong that Eddie has done to him. Both men see a disparity between what their morality tells them is *wrong* and what the law defines as *illegal*. Another of Alfieri's comments is germane here: he tells Eddie that 'the law is nature. The law is only a word for what has a right to happen' (p.66). But neither Eddie nor Marco can accept this, because to them (as to nearly everyone) their moral perspective *is* nature, and hence anything that does not fit in with it is *unnatural*.

The dislocation between what we will call *civil law* (that is, the legislated mandates of the society in question – here the United States of America) and some other perceived form of law, whether it is natural law, or the law of honour, appears in a number of ways throughout *A View from the Bridge*. Eddie sees a violation of natural law in the possibility of a 'homosexual' marrying his niece; Marco sees it as a violation of the law of honour that Eddie should be allowed to live after his betrayal; Marco intentionally transgresses American immigration laws to pursue a more basic law – that a man must feed his family (while Rodolpho transgresses them for reasons of his own); and, of course, Eddie and Beatrice eschew civil law in favour of family when they offer safe haven to Marco and Rodolpho. In a place like Red Hook, people have to make choices, and in much the same way that longshoremen would 'rather not get too close' (p.11) to a lawyer like Alfieri, they are inclined to favour the imperatives of what we might call 'local laws' to those of civil law.

No character is more beholden to 'local laws' than Eddie. His is a very small world, one of work, home and neighbourhood, a rigid world in which things are so clearly defined because they are so circumscribed. Eddie knows precisely what his standing is in his community and in his home; maintaining it is of the utmost importance to him. He knows what the rules are. His conflicts with other characters originate, at least to Eddie's mind, in their transgressions of these rules – in Catherine's precocious desires to get a job and fall in love, in Beatrice's refusal to 'respect' him properly, in Rodolpho's not acting like a 'man'. We are not straying from the topic of law and justice in discussing Eddie's *rules*, because to Eddie, such rules devolve out of what he considers to be natural laws.

The transgression of his rules by other characters most disturbs Eddie in the way it undermines that very certainty of his position, whether at home or in the neighbourhood, and this doubt is at the heart of everything he does. Eddie's obsession with Catherine may be the catalyst for his actions, but in the ensuing conflicts with other characters we learn a lot about the rigidity of his world view and about his capacity for self-deception. His demand for Beatrice's respect 'as the husband' is a reaction against something he cannot admit to himself – that in no longer having a sexual relationship with his wife, he is *failing* as a husband. Something similar occurs in Eddie's demand that Marco restores his 'name' to him in public. The crucial importance of maintaining his standing in the neighbourhood negates any realisation of guilt on Eddie's part; he goes so far as to accuse Marco and Rodolpho of betraying *him* (p.83).

Key point

Freud invented a term for this kind of denial: projection, a defence mechanism of the subconscious that cleanses the psyche of one's faults by shifting them onto other people. At home, Eddie's subconscious mind projects his own marital failings onto Beatrice; out in front of the neighbourhood, it projects his betrayal of a family member onto Marco.

The greatest case of projection occurs in Eddie's accusations against Rodolpho. As Alfieri suggests to him, Eddie's desire for Catherine is unnatural: it is not incest, but it goes against the natural order. Like a father, the guardian is supposed to love and support the child until she is old enough to choose her own mate. To try to keep her as a lover, or as some kind of captive in a perpetual childhood, is to offend against the laws of nature. Though never able to admit that such a desire for Catherine exists within him, Eddie's subconscious mind seems to be lashed by it. His own (repressed) awareness of the unnaturalness of this desire leads Eddie to accuse Rodolpho of homosexuality, which Eddie considers totally unnatural.

Here we have Eddie's dilemma. He is a man with an intricate set of rules dictating every aspect of his life, from the way a man should behave on the waterfront, to how a husband should be treated at home; yet his obsession with Catherine leads him to break the most important laws by which he has defined himself. Unable to accept this, he lashes out at everyone else, accusing them of his own faults and seeking justice where he knows, at least subconsciously, that he does not deserve it. Indeed, there is something fitting in the way Eddie seeks the redemption of his name from Marco. One could argue that what Eddie's subconscious really desires is relief from the burden of guilt it carries, and that relief, that justice, can only come with Eddie's death – as indeed it does, symbolically, on the blade of his own knife.

Watching the catastrophe

Key quotes

'MARCO: What can I do? The older [child] is sick in his chest. My wife – she feeds them from her own mouth. I tell you the truth, if I stay [in Italy] they will never grow up.' (p.29)

'EDDIE: And now I gotta sit in my own house and look at a son-of-a-bitch punk like that… [put] his dirty filthy hands on her like a goddam thief!' (p.49)

'ALFIERI: And I sat here many afternoons asking myself why, being an intelligent man, I was so powerless to stop it.' (p.50)

Alfieri is not the only character in this play forced to watch a catastrophe unfold before his eyes, nor is he the only one to feel powerless. The same thing can be said of Eddie, forced to watch Catherine fall in love with another man; of Beatrice, forced to watch as her husband destroys himself through his forbidden desires; of Marco, forced to contemplate his children starving in Italy. Though it is not quite true that Alfieri does nothing to intercede in Eddie's story (he offers advice to Eddie twice), the other characters do considerably more to effect some change in their personal catastrophe. Yet each of them fails just as surely as Alfieri fails. Looking at their individual dilemmas and the doomed remedies they conceive can tell us a lot about the play itself.

Beatrice's lack of power

The least powerful character in the play would have to be Beatrice. The catastrophe she witnesses is her husband's growing obsession with their niece Catherine. She cannot raise the subject directly with Eddie, but Beatrice does criticise him for an *effect* of this obsession – that he is not letting Catherine become an adult. Mostly she takes the matter up with Catherine, insisting that Catherine break Eddie's control over her by going out on her own. Rodolpho's arrival disrupts the status quo; while it does indeed make Catherine finally break Eddie's grip (albeit reluctantly, at least until she learns of his betrayal), Eddie's jealousy makes him lose control of his actions. There is nothing Beatrice can do except watch the tragedy unfold – one senses her resignation to her powerlessness when she says she is 'sick and tired of it' (p.68).

Only when it becomes clear that it will all end in bloodshed does Beatrice address Eddie's desires directly; by then it is too late. I suggested above that the couple's inability to communicate is partly responsible for the events that unfold, but judging by Eddie's response to what Beatrice says about his desire for Catherine – his agony and his denial (p.83) – it might be true that the matter was never something the two could 'discuss'. Beatrice's realisation of this is the true source of her powerlessness.

Marco's family

The catastrophe Marco must 'watch' happens offstage: the poverty and slow starvation of his children in Italy. Attempting to remedy the situation, he comes illegally to America. Who could blame him? Though he is a man of determination and strength, Marco finds himself in a position similar to Beatrice's; he cannot reverse the catastrophe by himself, but needs the help of his American cousins. His gratitude to Eddie and Beatrice in Act One reveals that he does not take their assistance for granted, but the ferocity of his feelings after Eddie informs on Marco and his brother reveals just how serious the matter is. Eddie has not simply withdrawn his support for Marco, he has destroyed Marco's chance to save his family, going from benefactor to murderer in the other's eyes. It is not surprising that Marco comes to destroy Eddie in revenge, but Eddie's death should not obscure the fact that Marco's attempt to prevent his own family's catastrophe has failed.

Eddie's assault on the natural order

Then there is Eddie. We know what happens when he intervenes to prevent the loss of Catherine to Rodolpho. Most interesting is the contrast between Eddie's dilemma and those of the other characters. Unlike Beatrice's catastrophe, or Marco's, Eddie's catastrophe is at one and the same time a figure of his imagination, and a reality too painful for him to address in its true form. He acts unconsciously against Rodolpho's taking Catherine away from him, without considering that Catherine was never his to begin with. But he cannot consciously acknowledge his real motivation, so his mind creates a different scenario: that he must save Catherine from a scheming homosexual.

Thus, Eddie's 'catastrophe' is a delusion masking a reality he cannot come to terms with. Beatrice and Marco each attempt to take action against a horrific possibility; Eddie turns those possibilities, and others, into reality because he takes action against what is right. If Marco and Beatrice require help to intervene as they try to forestall their catastrophes, Eddie is able to destroy everyone's hopes all by himself. Sadly, this may be the most realistic aspect of Miller's play.

If we contrast Eddie with Alfieri, we obtain a similar picture. The lawyer criticises himself for being unable to take a greater hand in swaying Eddie from his course. So he should, because to do so would be to help protect the natural order from Eddie's rampage. Eddie, by contrast, is trying to destroy what is right and natural, in the hope of preserving something unnatural. Eddie's frantic activity and Alfieri's introspective passivity are again depressingly realistic. One thinks of Yeats's lines from his poem 'The Second Coming': 'The best lack all conviction while the worst / Are full of passionate intensity'.

Love and jealousy

Key quotes

'BEATRICE: You think I'm jealous of you, honey?

CATHERINE: No! It's the first I thought of it.

BEATRICE: Well you should have thought of it before ... but I'm not.' (p.44)

'ALFIERI: [T]here is too much love for the daughter, there is too much love for the niece. Do you understand what I'm saying to you?' (p.48)

'CATHERINE: Eddie, I never meant to do nothing bad to you.' (p.84)

Love and jealousy are familiar bedfellows; the stronger we love, the stronger we feel the pull of jealousy (whether or not we actually recognise it as such). Jealousy is one of the great human torments: to be jealous is to be suspicious that something or someone we prize, perhaps above all others, will be taken from us, coldly, irreparably, by a callous rival. Any emotion can lead to pathological behaviour, of course; but jealousy is a destroyer that makes us believe we are about to be disfigured by loss. The paradox is tragic: if we do not love we do not become jealous. But who would want a life without love?

Beatrice tells Catherine she is not jealous of her. We should probably believe her; her problem is not that Catherine has inserted herself as a rival for Eddie's love, but that Eddie has placed Catherine there himself. Beatrice seems motivated not by jealousy, but by fear of the consequences that will come from Eddie's obsession.

It is in Eddie and Catherine's relationship that the play really explores this theme. A shallow reading might conclude that their relationship is simple: one of those cases where a platonic relationship becomes problematic because one person falls in love with the other (albeit with more severe consequences than average). But we are not shallow readers; Eddie and Catherine's relationship is much more complex than this, and as a result, more troubling. Again, we must not forget Eddie's original willingness to take on Beatrice's orphaned niece and love her as his own child. It is a case of an entirely proper and generous, even heroic, love becoming something very different.

The tension between platonic and sexual love

We tend to think of there being a distinct transformation from platonic love to sexual love, but I think we should consider it rather as the addition of a dimension. In Eddie's case we see a man struggling, unconsciously, with an enormous guilt about his new feelings for Catherine, yet old platonic feelings clearly remain; for example, in his wanting the best for her future, his pride in her achievements, the delight he takes in hearing her talk about her day. These aspects of his regard for her need not change just because he now sees her as a romantic object, yet Eddie's *guilt* taints these old feelings, distorts them into mere subjects for his jealousy. Admittedly, it is the mature person indeed who can move from platonic love to unrequited sexual love and still regard the relationship without bitterness. Eddie is not such a person, but he has the added burden of his enormous guilt: it stains his relationship, corrupts it, turns his love into a raging jealousy that he allows himself to believe is actually parental regard – looking out for Catherine's best interests.

Eddie's actions are deplorable, and his inability to own up to his feelings and confront them is only slightly less so. Yet in Eddie, Miller has given us a character crucified by jealousy, and we would have to be cold creatures indeed not to be moved by the spectacle. The stronger we love, the stronger our potential jealousy – and Eddie's jealousy is lethal. The most devastating aspect of *A View from the Bridge* is watching the emotion of jealousy poison what is portrayed as a noble and powerful love.

Catherine's love for Eddie

If we see Eddie as nothing more than a leering pervert, we will miss the point of the play. Catherine's dilemma is not all that different from Eddie's, though of course she is not *in love* with him and so does not feel the tear of jealousy as he does. But like Eddie, Catherine is confronted with the loss of the greatest love in her life to that point. She is able to see the sense in the requests Beatrice makes for her not to act like a child around Eddie any more, but Catherine bridles at what she suspects is *underneath* the request, a wish for her to remove herself from Eddie's life altogether. She says to Rodolpho: 'I'm supposed to turn around and make a stranger out of him? I don't know why I have to do that' (p.62). If theirs was a 'normal' parent-child relationship, there is no reason why Catherine *would* have to make a 'stranger' out of Eddie.

But Beatrice is right: Eddie's obsession with Catherine is so advanced that this is now the only solution. This does not make it any easier for Catherine; in her speech to Rodolpho from which I took the above quote, Catherine talks about Eddie almost as though *she*, rather than Beatrice, was his real wife. Does this suggest that there is indeed a sexual dimension to Catherine's regard for Eddie? We cannot exclude the possibility completely – what that means, basically, is that the issue is treated ambiguously enough in the text for a director to explore it in a production without having to make alterations or elisions.

Catherine and Eddie: one interpretation

Eddie and Catherine's relationship during the years between her adoption and her sexual maturity was based on a powerful and mutual love. It is easy to understand how a girl growing up without parents, in a house with two adults, might develop an unusually strong attachment to one of them. It is a little more difficult to assume that Eddie would have developed an equally strong attachment. Catherine is seventeen, Eddie is forty; this means that she came into their lives when Eddie and Beatrice were only in their early twenties, probably recently married and struggling. I suggest it would be far more likely that a man who had no blood relationship with the child would resent her as an added burden rather than love her. We should not dismiss Eddie's complaints about 'breaking his back' for Catherine even though he uses them to justify reprehensible actions. Rather, we should look at what is best in Eddie, his hard work and devotion to the baby that came unbidden into his life, to understand why he loved her so much. The Eddie who complains is the one whose opinions have been disfigured by his jealousy. The one who worked for her without complaining is the one who loved her despite it.

Some people regard platonic love as a relationship more shallow than sexual love. But this was not Plato's idea at all: the love that has come to bear his name was envisioned as the highest kind of love, genuine and pure, unencumbered by carnality and its 'low' instincts. We must resist the temptation to think that Eddie raised his feelings for Catherine to a higher level upon her sexual maturity. The truth is just the opposite; his desire for her lowers the relationship to mere physicality, and Eddie's shame is not, I think, unleavened by the realisation of what has been lost. If we follow the platonic model, we might interpret all of Eddie's actions in the play – the accusations, the betrayal, the lies, the bullying, the sexual intimidation (of Catherine and Rodolpho), the arguably suicidal challenge to Marco – as not just a natural progression of his jealousy, but the inevitable result of allowing physical desire to sully platonic love. Maybe that's what jealousy is.

Respect and honour

Key quotes

'EDDIE: I want my respect!' (p.68)

'MARCO: He knows such a promise is dishonourable.' (p.78)

'EDDIE: I want my name! [Rodolpho] didn't take my name; he's only a punk. Marco's got my name…' (p.82)

A great deal of importance is placed on individual respect in *A View from the Bridge*. Like many of the characters, Eddie lives by a certain code – there is a strong suggestion that it goes back to his family's origins in Sicily. One of the demands of his code is that as head of the family he is entitled to respect from his wife, including respect for his decisions, even on matters of opinion: 'A wife is supposed to believe the husband... If I tell you [Rodolpho] ain't right don't tell me he is right' (p.69). In other words, in Eddie's world, 'respect' means that his word is law, at least to his wife, no matter how erroneous or bigoted it may be. Eddie also demands respect in other quarters: he reprimands Rodolpho for taking Catherine out without seeking Eddie's approval first. If this is a very old-fashioned request, even for the 1950s, it is part of Eddie's strategy of alienating Rodolpho from Catherine.

Showing respect for Catherine

Catherine insists that Rodolpho *is* showing proper respect for her, so it is interesting that this is the issue Rodolpho chastises Eddie about when the latter forces his kiss on Catherine: 'Stop that! Have respect for her!' (p.64). Eddie's same behaviour towards Rodolpho is listed by Marco as one of his grudges against Eddie ('He degraded my brother', p.79) – in other words, in both cases, Eddie is sinning against the laws of individual respect. It should be pointed out that when Rodolpho coaxes Catherine into the bedroom to have sex (at the very first opportunity), audiences of 1955 might have been more inclined than us to see justification in Eddie's claims against him. It is no coincidence that the forced kisses of Catherine and Rodolpho come immediately after Eddie breaks in on their seclusion.

A duel or a vendetta?

In the old code under which Eddie and the other characters live, a lack of respect must be settled by some expression of honour. The climax of the play, the fight between Eddie and Marco, can be thought of as a kind of duel. Both men seek to redress stains against their honour. To Marco it would be dishonourable to allow Eddie to live after he has betrayed him to the Immigration Bureau. Marco's commitment to his code of honour can be measured both by the depth of his gratitude to Eddie upon his and Rodolpho's arrival and, conversely, by the intensity of his hatred after Eddie's betrayal. Eddie is fighting to restore his position in the community; Marco has stolen his 'name' and it is a point of honour that he recovers it, forcibly if necessary.

Indeed, Eddie seems to work himself into the correct fighting mood by ticking off a list, in front of the whole neighbourhood, of the ways that the two brothers have allegedly abused Eddie's generosity. In past centuries, people duelled as a way of working out such conflicts of honour. But not all duels came to bloodshed; there were recourses by which both parties could agree to call it off, their very willingness to *meet* in a duel being considered enough to expunge the doubts on their honour. Many more duels were walked away from, honourably, than were fought.

Unfortunately, there can be no such conclusion in *A View from the Bridge*; Marco's wound is too deep, and Eddie's inability to come to terms with the reasons for his betrayal precludes his ability to accept responsibility for it. One struggles to see Eddie and Marco as nineteenth-century duellists, anyway (each with his cape and pistol). Their hostility has more of the feeling of the vendetta, the merciless blood feuds between families in southern Italy and Corsica, usually based on revenge for the murder of a family member. Each man is the head of a family that, rightly or wrongly, he sees as under attack by the other. The association between the Americans and their Italian cousins begins gracefully in *A View from the Bridge*, with generosity, self-sacrifice and honour; by the end it degenerates into a new-world vendetta that can only be settled with blood.

QUESTIONS & ANSWERS

Essay writing – an overview

An essay is a formal and serious piece of writing that presents your point of view on the text, usually in response to a given essay topic. Your 'point of view' in an essay is your interpretation of the meaning of the text's language, structure, characters, situations and events, supported by detailed analysis of textual evidence.

Analyse – don't summarise

In your essays it is important to avoid simply summarising what happens in a text:

- A **summary** is a description or paraphrase (retelling in different words) of the characters and events. For example: 'Macbeth has a horrifying vision of a dagger dripping with blood before he goes to murder King Duncan'.
- An **analysis** is an explanation of the real meaning or significance that lies 'beneath' the text's words (and images, for a film). For example: 'Macbeth's vision of a bloody dagger shows how deeply uneasy he is about the violent act he is contemplating – as well as his sense that supernatural forces are impelling him to act'.

A limited amount of summary is sometimes necessary to let your reader know which part of the text you wish to discuss. However, always keep this to a minimum and follow it immediately with your analysis (explanation) of what this part of the text is really telling us.

Plan your essay

Carefully plan your essay so that you have a clear idea of what you are going to say. The plan ensures that your ideas flow logically, that your argument remains consistent and that you stay on the topic. An essay plan should be a list of **brief dot points** – no more than half a page.

- Include your central argument or main contention – a concise statement (usually in a single sentence) of your overall response to the topic. See 'Analysing a sample topic' for guidelines on how to formulate a main contention.
- Write three or four dot points for each paragraph indicating the main idea and evidence/examples from the text. Note that in your essay you will need to expand on these points and analyse the evidence.

Structure your essay

An essay is a complete, self-contained piece of writing. It has a clear beginning (the introduction), middle (several body paragraphs) and end (the last paragraph or conclusion). It must also have a central argument that runs throughout, linking each paragraph to form a coherent whole. See examples of introductions and conclusions in the 'Analysing a sample topic' and 'Sample answer' sections.

The introduction establishes your overall response to the topic. It includes your main contention and outlines the main evidence you will refer to in the course of the essay. Write your introduction *after* you have done a plan and *before* you write the rest of the essay.

The body paragraphs argue your case – they present evidence from the text and explain how this evidence supports your argument. Each body paragraph needs:

- a strong **topic sentence** (usually the first sentence) that states the main point being made in the paragraph
- **evidence** from the text, including some brief quotations
- **analysis** of the textual evidence explaining its significance and explanation of how it supports your argument
- **links back to the topic** in one or more statements, usually towards the end of the paragraph.

Connect the body paragraphs so that your discussion flows smoothly. Use some linking words and phrases like 'similarly' and 'on the other hand', though don't start every paragraph like this. Another strategy is to use a significant word from the last sentence of one paragraph in the first sentence of the next. Use key terms from the topic – or synonyms for them – throughout, so the relevance of your discussion to the topic is always clear.

The conclusion ties everything together and finishes the essay. It includes strong statements that emphasise your central argument and provide a clear response to the topic.

Avoid simply restating the points made earlier in the essay – this will end on a very flat note and imply that you have run out of ideas and vocabulary. The conclusion is meant to be a logical extension of what you have written, not just a repetition or summary of it. Writing an effective conclusion can be a challenge. Try using these tips:

- Start by linking back to the final sentence of the second-last paragraph – this helps your writing to 'flow', rather than just leaping back to your main contention straight away.
- Use synonyms and expressions with equivalent meanings to vary your vocabulary. This allows you to reinforce your line of argument without being repetitive.
- When planning your essay, think of one or two broad statements or observations about the text's wider meaning. These should be related to the topic and your overall argument. Keep them for the conclusion, since they will give you something 'new' to say but still follow logically from your discussion. The introduction will be focused on the topic, but the conclusion can present a wider view of the text.

Essay topics

1 'He allowed himself to be wholly known.' Is Alfieri's assessment of Eddie an accurate one?

2 'You're a baby, you don't understand these things.' Is Catherine really as naive as Eddie says she is?

3 'You can quicker get back a million dollars that was stole than a word that you gave away.' It is only when Eddie goes back on his word that he realises its true value. Discuss.

4 'Eddie Carbone never expected to have a destiny.' Eddie's destiny is not predetermined; he forges it himself. Do you agree?

5 Eddie is a flawed character whose impotence 'in the bed' is symptomatic of his frustration in interacting with others. Do you agree?

6 'Justice is very important here.' *A View from the Bridge* shows that, while justice is important, it is not always the same thing as the law. Discuss.

7 'Every man's got somebody he loves, heh? But sometimes ... there's too much.' *A View from the Bridge* reveals that when love is excessive it has destructive consequences. Discuss.

8 'I knew where he was heading for ... I was so powerless to stop it.' *A View from the Bridge* shows that, ultimately, individuals must take responsibility for their own fates. Discuss.

9 'I want my respect, Beatrice, and you know what I'm talkin' about.' *A View from the Bridge* suggests that respect can never be taken, only given. Discuss.

10 'Even those who understand will turn against you, even the ones who feel the same will despise you.' *A View from the Bridge* illustrates the power of community attitudes to control individual fates. Discuss.

Analysing a sample topic

'Every man's got somebody that he loves, heh? But sometimes ... there's too much.' *A View from the Bridge* reveals that when love is excessive it has destructive consequences. Discuss.

- The question asks you to discuss *A View from the Bridge* in its entirety. This means that you will need to look at a number of examples of love in the play, rather than focus on one. The term 'love' is general and abstract; in order to be able to discuss specific elements of the play, you will need to think about relationships between characters.
- Which characters love other characters? As the quote suggests, everyone loves someone: Eddie loves Catherine, Beatrice loves Eddie, Catherine and Rodolpho love each other, Catherine loves →

Eddie, Marco loves his family. There are many relationships to choose from; you must select evidence from the text that relates clearly to the topic's contention, and to its key terms 'excessive' and 'destructive'.

- In this topic, the contention adds to the content of the quote by introducing the notion of love as a destructive force. You must decide whether to agree, disagree or partially agree / disagree with the contention.
- You should be able to recognise that the quote is from a speech by Alfieri, and refers to Eddie's improper love for Catherine. This relationship is clearly the most complicated and the most obvious to consider in terms of love being *excessive*, so will prove the richest for discussion. But before formulating your arguments about it, decide which other relationships you want to discuss. I would recommend choosing two or three others, let's say Catherine's love for Eddie, as it will provide an excellent contrast with your main example; Beatrice's love for Eddie; and Marco's love for his wife and children.
- Before writing the essay itself, do some brainstorming about each of the examples you will discuss. Without the pressure of writing coherent and grammatically correct sentences, spend five or ten minutes making lists on scrap paper of everything you know about the relationships in question. When you have done this, go through what you have and eliminate all but the strongest and most interesting arguments for each.
- You are nearly ready to write. Think about what you have. Look for the connecting threads between the individual ideas you have come up with. Are these connecting ideas consistent with the contention that excessive love is destructive? Or do they contradict it – by suggesting, for instance, that there is no such thing as excessive love, only misguided love?
- Take another few minutes to create a brief outline: decide which facts you will discuss and in what order. Simply lining up your arguments in this way can provide you with insight into the case you would like to make. It is much easier to focus on a particular argument when

your mind is not burdened by keeping track of all the other arguments you need to make. Having an outline will relieve this burden.

- Before writing, look again at the question – what else is there to assist you in formulating your argument? The last part of Alfieri's statement ('But sometimes... there's too much') is surely the 'entry point' for your discussion of Eddie's love for Catherine, a love that has broken through the acceptable boundaries for a guardian and his charge to become something else.
- As you write about each relationship, remember that the examiners are looking primarily to see that you *know the play* and that you can *formulate coherent arguments* about it. Instead of only *saying* that Eddie's desire for Catherine clouds his ability to make rational judgements (for instance), give specific examples (for example, his judgement that Rodolpho is homosexual).
- Know what your conclusion is about each relationship and write in such a way that there is an obvious progression towards it. Arguments are constructed one brick at a time. These conclusions need not be earthshaking revelations; it is more important that you make your argument strong by offering plenty of supporting evidence than that you make a *unique* argument.
- Your conclusion should reiterate your overall argument about what *A View from the Bridge* suggests to you about human behaviour, and in particular about the intensities and consequences of love. This conclusion might entail a recognition, in disagreement with the contention, that there is no single idea that Miller is trying to convey about love. In an essay that has gone into depth about a number of love relationships in the play and has demonstrated how different they are, this will be judged a mature and well-founded conclusion; an essay that offers little such justification for its argument will be less successful.
- What is important is not so much *what* your conclusions are, as whether you have *demonstrated the case*, with meaningful analysis of specific examples from the play.

SAMPLE ANSWER

Eddie is a flawed character whose impotence 'in the bed' is symptomatic of his frustration in interacting with others. Do you agree?

A View from the Bridge highlights the potential for disaster when frustration and impotence govern our interactions with others. Eddie Carbone's frustration and impotence are evident on two levels. He is sexually frustrated because of his desire for his niece, Catherine. In turn, this results in his disinclination for marital relations with his wife, Beatrice. Eddie is also frustrated and angered in his attempts to prevent outcomes which he does not desire, but over which he has no control. Impotence also has sexual connotations, suggesting a physical incapacity, but in more general terms it implies a lack of power and control over one's life. Eddie's sexual frustration and impotence clearly reflect an inability to cope, and highlight his lack of control over his life.

It could argued that what Eddie does not feel like doing 'in the bed' is more a consequence of his lack of desire for Beatrice rather than a lack of ability to perform what is required of him as a husband. Beatrice is also frustrated, pointing out that 'it's almost three months' and asking Eddie, 'when am I gonna be a wife again?' Yet for Eddie, desire is crucial and his deeply repressed sexual desire for Catherine impedes his ability to fulfil his role as a husband, both 'in the bed' and in the marriage. He is critical and unsupportive of Beatrice, even before the arrival of Marco and Rodolpho, 'strangely' and resentfully dismissing her opinions because '[she] never worked in [her] life', and criticising her because 'she's got too big a heart'. Given Beatrice's almost slavish devotion to Eddie, this seems unreasonable and reveals a festering anger in Eddie, born of impotence and dissatisfaction. His often churlish behaviour exposes the flaws in his character: he is passionate, inflexible and ill-equipped to deal with frustration.

As Catherine's protector, Eddie wants 'the best' for her but is powerless to enforce his will when he fears that she is acting unwisely. He disapproves of Catherine's 'too short' skirt and warns her against being 'too friendly' with the longshoremen. Alarmed by the 'heads turnin' like windmills' when she walks down the street, Eddie tries to prolong Catherine's childhood, calling her a 'baby' and insisting she 'finish school'. Yet his repressed desire for her demonstrates his failure to do so and affects all his attempts to guide and counsel her. Eddie's simmering anger at his inability to fulfil his desires dominates family interactions, which often revolve around the need to placate him. Beatrice is adept at soothing him; she calls him an 'angel' for sheltering her cousins and deftly changes the subject when she anticipates tension, amusing Eddie with a reminiscence about spiders in a coffee shipment. Catherine, too knows how to please Eddie; she eagerly promises to 'fix up the whole house' with her first pay. These attempts to defuse Eddie's anger reveal both Beatrice's and Catherine's awareness of Eddie's frustration, although Beatrice is more acutely aware of its source. It is she who recognises most clearly the flaws in Eddie's character, which Alfieri also observes. He quickly recognises Eddie's passionate and inflexible nature, seeing him as 'a dark figure walking down a hall' and knowing 'where he was going to end'.

Eddie's aggravation extends most noticeably to his inability to dampen Catherine's interest in Rodolpho. He believes that Rodolpho is using Catherine as a 'passport', but articulating his concerns merely exacerbates the situation; Catherine becomes defensive, angrily insisting that Rodolpho 'loves [her]'. Frustrated and disempowered by Alfieri's blunt assertion that he has 'no rights' and 'cannot stop' Catherine's marriage to Rodolpho, Eddie calls on a higher power: the Immigration Bureau. Yet ironically, Eddie places himself at the mercy of an even more powerful force: that of an ancient code of family honour which Eddie has betrayed and which Marco relentlessly enforces. Both Eddie and Marco know that 'all the law is not in a book' and that Eddie must pay the ultimate price for his inability to deal with his frustration and impotence.

Eddie's bitter disappointment over Catherine's and Rodolpho's relationship has almost as much to do with his dislike of Rodolpho as it does with his desire for Catherine. Despite the fact 'if a prince came', he would not be good enough, in Eddie's eyes, Rodolpho is particularly unsuitable, perhaps because he is the antithesis of Eddie, who is described as 'forty', 'husky' and 'slightly overweight'. He is of Sicilian descent, presumably 'dark' like Marco, and relatively taciturn by nature. Rodolpho, by contrast, is young, handsome, blond and exuberant. Eddie regards him with deep suspicion, labelling him a 'thief' and a 'punk'. Given Eddie's desire for Catherine, her attraction to someone so entirely unlike him is perhaps humiliating. Eddie's caustic comment: 'Of him? Boy, you don't think much of me', in response to Beatrice's accusation that he is 'jealous', is significant. He does not deny a capacity for jealousy of Catherine's suitors but utterly dismisses Rodolpho's validity as a rival. Ironically, it is Rodolpho whose sexual desire for Catherine is fulfilled, while Eddie remains frustrated and impotent. His outrage over Rodolpho's seduction of Catherine prompts Eddie to make the fatal call to the Immigration Bureau.

Miller's play shows sexual desire to be a powerful force that can have unforeseen and far-reaching effects. Eddie Carbone's sexual frustration and impotence highlight his inability to deal with forces beyond his control. He is a flawed character who struggles against his own incestuous desires, and suffers the inevitable consequences.

REFERENCES & READING

Text

Miller, Arthur 2000, *A View from the Bridge* and *All My Sons*, Penguin, London.

Reference

Miller, Arthur 1977, *A View from the Bridge*, Penguin, New York.

Further reading

Bigsby, Christopher (ed.) 1990, *Arthur Miller and Company*, Methuen Drama (in association with the Arthur Miller Centre for American Studies), London.

Bigsby, Christopher (ed.) 1997, *The Cambridge Companion to Arthur Miller*, Cambridge University Press, Cambridge.

Corrigan, Robert W (ed.) 1969, *Arthur Miller: A Collection of Critical Essays*, Prentice-Hall, Englewood Cliffs, NJ.

Gottfried, Martin 2003, *Arthur Miller: A Life*, Faber, London.

Hayman, Ronald 1972, *Arthur Miller*, Ungar, New York.

Martin, Robert (ed.) 1982, *Arthur Miller: New Perspectives*, Prentice-Hall, Englewood Cliffs, NJ.

Martin, Robert (ed.) 1978, *The Theater Essays of Arthur Miller*, Viking, New York.

Miller, Arthur 2001, *On Politics and the Art of Acting*, Viking, New York.

Schlueter, June and Flanagan, James K 1987, *Arthur Miller*, Ungar, New York.

Adaptations

A View from the Bridge was made into a film in 1962, directed by Sidney Lumet (Produzione Intercontinentali; Transcontinental); it is also an opera by William Bolcom.